MW00389172

ADVANCE PRAISE FOR *PEOPLE FIRST*

"Don't miss reading *People First*. All the great companies I've worked with over the years think their people are their #1 customer. As a result, as the Carpenters emphasize, they LOVE on their people. If you want evidence that 'profit is the applause you get for taking good care of your people so they will take good care of your customers,' read this book. Thanks Three and Jackie."
—Ken Blanchard, Co-author of *The One Minute Manager* and *Servant Leadership in Action*

"The 5 steps in *People First* are an inspirational path to creating a thriving organization. You won't just read it; you'll use it…and love it!"
—Walt Rakowich, Former CEO, Prologis

"How do you ensure team engagement and customer experience success? Three and Jackie Carpenter have the answers and provide them in a straightforward, practical, and memorable way. *People First* is for everyone who is willing to love and serve others in pursuit of meteoric business and personal success. Run to the counter or click 'buy now' to access this transformative, refreshing, and much-needed resource."
—Joseph Michelli, Ph.D., Certified Customer Experience Consultant, *New York Times* #1 bestselling author of books like *Stronger Through Adversity, The New Gold Standard,* and *The Starbucks Experience*

"In *People First*, Three and Jackie deliver practical and implementable leadership concepts. This is an excellent read about building and leading passionate teams. It is the key to boosting productivity and results in any organization."
—Kim Pasquale, SVP, Member Engagement, Club Management Association of America

THE 5 STEPS TO PURE HUMAN CONNECTION
AND A THRIVING ORGANIZATION

PEOPLE F1RST

THREE CARPENTER and **JACKIE CARPENTER**

A POST HILL PRESS BOOK
ISBN: 978-1-63758-026-4
ISBN (eBook): 978-1-63758-027-1

People First:
The 5 Steps to Pure Human Connection and a Thriving Organization
© 2021 by Three Carpenter and Jackie Carpenter
All Rights Reserved

Author photo by Maddy Heskett
Illustrations by Marisa Carioscia

Elephant Illustration by Benjamin Vincent

Post Hill Press
New York • Nashville
posthillpress.com

Published in the United States of America
1 2 3 4 5 6 7 8 9 10

TABLE OF CONTENTS

TOMMY SPAULDING

What is the definition of a broken record? If you google the words "broken record," you get the literal definition: a damaged record that repeats part of a recording over and over again.

I have been blessed to study and teach leadership—particularly servant leadership—for nearly thirty years. I've had the honor of working with thousands of companies to develop their leaders and build successful cultures. Let's call these organizations Company A. They have a culture that puts people over profits. They hire and train their people to be heart-led leaders. They are people oriented and results driven. And their employees feel loved, trusted, valued, and appreciated.

Unfortunately, though, there are too many companies out there that put profits over their people. Let's call them Company B. Their leaders are self-serving. Their cultures are quite often cancerous. Their employees are desperate for stronger leadership and suffocating under their workload because they are not valued within the organization. When a company only cares about profits, its people are miserable, the culture is toxic, turnover is higher, and success is fleeting. I hear this story over and over again. Company B organizations, to put it simply, are a broken record—stuck in a repeat pattern of a bad or indifferent behavior towards employees.

Yet sadly, there are more Company Bs than Company As. I have dedicated my professional life to change this broken record. It's why I teach youth and leadership teams around the world that there is a different way to lead. There is a different leadership philosophy that truly values people. I call it Heart-Led Leadership.

My friends Three & Jackie Carpenter call it People First!

For far too long, employees have been thought of as tools to build profits. But what if employees were seen as people first—as human beings with needs, feelings, and dreams? What if employees were cared for, nurtured, and loved by their supervisors, managers, and executives? When business leaders get out of their own way and boldly lead with their people's best interests in mind (not their own), that is when servant leadership is taken to a whole new level.

People First is a mindset, a philosophy, and a conscious practice that creates the kind of company culture where employees *want* to go to work, not feel like they *have* to go to work. It's invigorating, not suffocating, because it creates teams of people who are working together with passion and purpose.

I have known Three & Jackie for well over a decade. They have volunteered at our National Leadership Academy youth program (www.nationalleadershipacademy.org), they have become professional peers, and they are dear and lifelong friends of my wife, Jill, and me. Three, Jackie, and I sing from the same score sheet—we understand that by loving and serving our people, organizations not only flourish, they produce better results in the long term. It is not love *or* results; it is love-driven results.

Three and Jackie are the opposite of a broken record. They are relatable and real. You can feel their contagious energy and passion for people as they explain how to build up employees, how to create loyal team members, and how to generate better organizational results through the People First mindset. They take you on a transformational journey from a transactional work environment (a broken record) to an upbeat, energetic culture where employees are connected, engaged, and working together as a unified team. The steps listed in the pages before you are actionable, easy to understand, and most importantly, they work!

I love this book because Three and Jackie don't just tell you *why* loving your employees is powerful, they show you *how* to love your employees. Read this book and let's stop the broken record of self-serving behavior and toxic leadership. People first matters! And believe me, when you get it right, it will be music to your ears.

CHAPTER 1:

INTRODUCTION

"If your actions create a legacy that inspires others
to dream more, learn more, do more and become
more, then, you are an excellent leader."
—Dolly Parton

Wouldn't it be amazing if employees came to work every day excited, happy, and eager to do their best? What if your employees loved their jobs so much that positions with your company were highly coveted? How awesome would it be if your employees were fully engaged and ready to fully contribute every day? What could be possible for your organization if this were all true?

Does it sound like a fantasy? Well…maybe it's not. We believe you can develop loyal employees who take ownership of their jobs and stick around, producing long-term value for your company, all while operating with excellence. We believe it because we've seen it; we've lived it. The truth is that if you create a situation where your employees are winning, your company will be winning too.

Our careers have been in the niche industry of private clubs—country clubs, golf clubs, city clubs, and so forth—where members spend hundreds of thousands of dollars just to be able to walk in the doors and take part in the amenities, activities, and events our clubs offer. In an industry where customer expectations are the absolute highest possible, we've been able to create teams that flourish.

First of all, yes, my name is Three. I was born a third and from the day of my birth, my parents called me Three, a sort of permanent nickname. It was one of the best gifts my parents could have given me because it inspired my unique way of thinking and my ability to stand out from the crowd. I'm the only Three I've ever met! This fueled my capacity to think, act, and lead differently too.

When I was twelve, I began working at my little hometown country club that happened to be fifty feet from the door of my childhood home. I officially got paid to work when I was fourteen, and at sixteen, I trained with the club's new head golf professional. At twenty-three, I had landed the general manager job. I realized at a very young age that I was blessed with a natural ability to lead others, yet I quickly discovered my leadership style was very different from others in that role.

Like me, Jackie began working in the hospitality industry when she was young. She was essentially managing her small hometown bar/restaurant when she was nineteen, and by the time she was twenty-four, she was overseeing a team of nearly three hundred employees at one of the most exclusive clubs in the country. Jackie and I worked together for several years and made a great team because I was the high-level visionary, and she was the best operator and implementer I've ever known. But long before we were married, we discovered our passion, energy, and genuine care for others were what made us a dynamic duo.

Over the years, we have worked at elite private clubs across the country and had some incredible experiences. But what makes us the most proud of our achievements are the accomplishments of those we've helped along the way. We've received dozens of letters, calls, and messages from former employees over the years that document how their lives were positively impacted by their time at our clubs. From telling us how they learned a great deal about leadership to thanking us for genuinely believing in them, it is humbling to know how much we've influenced others simply by paying attention to them. That is the reason we are writing this book.

Let's be clear, though: we aren't the CEOs of Google. We did not run a Fortune 500 company or manage thousands of people every day. We are normal people running average-sized businesses. So if we can do it, so can you. Yes, the contents of this book can indeed spark change in large organizations, but it can also be implemented at the local car dealership or a small-town florist shop. The results are the same, because when you support, educate, and love your employees enough to help them succeed, your company will benefit as well.

The business world has been poorly programmed to believe that employees are just cogs in a machine, nothing more than tools used to build a profit. After years researching and developing a process that supports employees at every phase of their career, Jackie and I made an incredible discovery. The way we treated our employees and the environment we created at our clubs, things we thought were what most successful companies were doing too, was not the norm in most organizations. In fact, we were amazed to find that our mode of operation was actually very rare.

We've poured our souls into this book because we want to shift the way the business world functions. We want employers of all sizes to stop thinking with a churn 'em and burn 'em mentality because employees are a dime a dozen. We want companies to look at employees as precious resources that must be treasured and nurtured because it is the right way to treat people! And living by this code is the only way to achieve lasting success.

This book is written for HR departments, managers, owners, leaders, and line-level employees who aspire to move up the ranks. You can apply the principles in this book at various levels and change the fabric of the organization at its core. We have done this on a smaller entrepreneurial scale. We came up with a program that seems to have worked, and we've implemented it at our clubs over the years. It changed those organizations and the people involved. Because of that, we want to share it with you.

One of the signature elements of this book is genuinely loving employees. Love, in business!?! Yes! That is exactly what we are doing. This isn't the normal language in business. We were always scared to use that word, but our good friend and bestselling author Tommy Spaulding preaches that managers must have servant hearts and lead their people with love (customers, employees, and the community). His book, *The Heart-Led Leader*, validated our belief that love in business can absolutely transform an organization. But we know the core of it all starts with your people, your *employees*. And the chapters ahead don't just tell you WHY you should love your employees; they show you HOW to love your employees. It took us four years to dissect our approach, define our beliefs, and document our behaviors to create a model that any business leader can replicate in any organization, no matter the size, and see positive change.

When we started writing this book, the economy was booming and the labor pool was continuing to tighten. It was an employees' world, with employers struggling to find and retain talented workers. Then the COVID-19 crisis hit. Suddenly thousands of businesses were closed, entire industries were at a standstill, and millions of people were out of work. The pandemic forced us to work, think, and operate differently. People experienced numerous challenges: trying to find a job, working from home, homeschooling children while working from home, adapting to a rapidly changing marketplace, and working on the front lines. We saw each other's pain points, and more than ever we ached for human connection. Employers must recognize that the human element in business is more important than ever! The pandemic changed the structure of the work environment, and although many examples in this book took place in a physical work environment, they still apply to a remote or altered work environment because People First really hasn't changed. And regardless of good or bad economic times, employees are the heart of every business.

Today's business world is evolving, but it has a long way to go. Whether in good economic times or bad, it is no secret that employees have been disengaged from their work. Gallup conducted a comprehensive survey of the US workplace in 2017. The report from thirty-one million respondents found that "the old ways of managing employees just aren't working and change isn't optional."[1] We've heard this anecdotally from others over the years as well. At a meeting of the Business Roundtable in 2019, Jamie Dimon, the chairman and CEO of JPMorgan Chase, vowed that the chief executives from 192 large companies were committed to delivering value to American workers for the future success of the organizations, their communities, and the country as a whole.[2] No longer can the primary goal of corporations be maximizing shareholder profits! The Business Roundtable affirmed the shift in culture the business world must make. In order to create a sustainable future, companies must establish healthy work environments that support the growth of employees and promote the betterment of their communities. The fact that this is the main focus of such an influential group speaks to the importance of this issue.

We've got to come together and prioritize what really matters in our organizations—our people! This book will teach you the art of creating a business that is not just employee-centric but one where executives and employees are joined in partnership. Even in the challenging times we've recently faced, creating this kind of culture has proven to be beneficial for the people and advantageous for the bottom line as well. We've designed this book to be all-encompassing for employers and will walk through every step of the employee life cycle, from recruitment to hiring to training to retention. From our extensive research, we know there are thousands of articles and dozens of books filled with advice for business leaders. Topics range from key questions to ask during interviews, to giving actionable feedback on performance, to creating a positive work culture; yet we found there wasn't one comprehensive approach. That's why this book is different.

When you look at the whole picture, it may be overwhelming to think about all the changes that need to be made in your company. It will be a process, and it won't happen overnight. But you have to start somewhere and build from there.

"HOW DO YOU EAT AN ELEPHANT?...ONE BITE AT A TIME."

A few years back, I had an artist draw me a picture of a man eating an elephant. It's hanging in my office as a constant reminder that change is slow. I want things fixed immediately, but this image helps me remember that the only way to eat an elephant—or make big organizational changes—is one bite at a time. Don't be overwhelmed—be focused!

Are you ready to get started?

Great! But before you do…we have one caveat. This book is not about us. We just feel compelled to share our message, and in doing so, we share our stories and experiences. Be prepared to dive deep into yourself, because this book is really about YOU. How you act. How you think. How you treat coworkers. How you prioritize job duties. And much more.

So turn the page and join us on this journey! Dig in to engage on a whole new level! It's time to jump off the struggle bus and forge the path ahead to a thriving organization.

CHAPTER 2:

DISCONNECTION

"When we strive to be become better than we are,
everything around us becomes better too."
—Paulo Coelho

I was confidently sitting at the end of the table in the first job interview of my life. It was 1992, and I was interviewing for the general manager's position at my small hometown country club where I had grown up. As members around the table questioned my ability to distinguish between being an employee rather than a child of a member, I quickly realized that I wasn't their optimal choice for the position. It was the answer to the next question, though, that accidentally propelled my career forward in ways I didn't yet understand.

"Three, what will you do as the leader of our club?"

Having grown up at this country club, I had always wondered what it might be like to run the club one day. So I was fully prepared for this tough question. A little nervous, I took a deep breath and said, "Well, I'm going to change the attitude and morale of the staff, the members, and the community. First, I'll create an environment where employees are respected and where they enjoy working. Next, I'll show our members that belonging to this club can enhance their lives and the lives of their families. Thirdly, I'll work to make sure the club is seen in a positive light by those in our community."

With that answer, I won over the interview committee and was offered the job! The answer to that question worked so well that a few years later when I was interviewing for the general manager position at an even bigger club, I used the same answer. I was all but patting myself on the back, waiting for their applause and nods of approval, when the gentleman on my left said, "Three, I know you can have an impact on our staff, and I can even get to the fact that you'd be able to impact the attitude and morale of our membership, but just exactly how are you going to change the perception of our club in the community?"

I sat quiet for a minute to respond as thoughtfully as possible and said, "Well, sir, you've discovered my secret. The truth is that I'm only really going to focus on the first thing, the staff. The employees will exceed member expectations and create a place where they are proud to belong. Members will be so pleased and impressed with what we are doing that they will go around telling others in the community about our club, ultimately creating a positive image of us within our city."

I landed that job too. But not because of some answer that sounded good in the interview room. It was because I had a vision for what I was going to do and a plan for how I was going to execute it. I didn't know it at the time, but what I was really saying was I was going to create a positive work culture. I focused first and foremost on the employees, their attitude, and morale; and as a result, the members and the community perceived the club in a more favorable light.

Many believe that the most important people in any business are the customers, because without them, you have nothing. While that is true, I have always believed that the most important people in any organization are the employees. They are the ones who interact with the customers. They are the people who build the products and provide services. They are the ones who make small decisions that add up to big dollars. Employees are the lifeblood of a business, and without them, you would have no customers! We agree wholeheartedly with Richard Branson, the founder of the Virgin Group, who says, "Take care of your employees and they'll take care of your business."

When bosses treat employees like objects, it's often because of a lack of managerial training, a lack of awareness, or an inability to see or understand the ramifications of their actions. Employees are people, not things. Treating employees like human beings who have thoughts, feelings, and needs is what we call *People First*. To us, it's all about putting our people first, and in fact, it's the core of everything we do. Every person desires to feel valued and respected, so shouldn't we be creating this kind of environment in our organizations? You know the saying "employees don't quit jobs, they quit bosses"? A 2018 study about Facebook supports this theory, but not in the way you may think. The study found the reasons employees were leaving was because "their job wasn't enjoyable, their strengths weren't being used and they weren't growing their careers." Ultimately, who is responsible for designing jobs and managing employee strengths and development? Managers.[3] So if we can teach all our leaders, including line or department managers and supervisors, to first see the person—their needs, feelings, strengths, and passions—and not the position—the title, role, or job duties—then we can create more caring and productive work environments.

Choosing a People First approach is the first step in sparking organizational change and creating positive work cultures. Establishing a workplace where coworkers treat each other with dignity and respect, and where trust and kindness are palpable, is essential for avoiding high employee turnover that costs businesses time and money. When people enjoy their work environment and feel appreciated and needed, they are much more likely to be engaged in their jobs, stay at their companies, and produce better results. An extensive eleven-year study published in a *Forbes* article noted the importance of organizational culture. It found that companies that encouraged leadership initiative and highly appreciated their employees produced *four times* more revenue in the eleven-year span than companies without this kind of culture.[4]

GOOD INTENTIONS

Today we are living in a tech-obsessed world where the belief is that technology is the solution for efficiency in the workplace. We sit in our workspaces and primarily communicate via emails, text messages, Slack, and other apps, often competing with our ability to really connect with others at work. While technological advancement has improved workplace productivity to an extent, in the last decade human development—*personal development*—has been sacrificed for technological development. We've been so distracted by technology that we lost our ability to focus on what's most important—*our people*!

Some years ago, Jackie was recruited to work as a business development professional for a private club in Nashville. The position was new to the company and the role was new to Jackie, one she had little experience in. Recruiting new members, building private event business, and seeking corporate partnerships were all things Jackie understood but had never actually done before. She was well versed in private clubs yet expressed that she would need the proper guidance and training, especially at the outset. The executive recruiting her assured Jackie he would make introductions to key business targets, attend meetings, and schedule biweekly sessions to coach her and help develop her skills. When Jackie heard he was also a business coach and mentor for other executives, she felt confident that she would be receiving the necessary support to succeed in this new role.

She accepted the position but resigned less than a year later. After months of frustration and floundering, Jackie felt hung out to dry. Only one biweekly coaching session happened in eleven months, and the executive all but ignored her. The only time he made a point to talk to her was when he critically complained about her progress and membership numbers. What Jackie thought would be an opportunity to advance her skills and personal development turned into utter disappointment, so she left.

Unfortunately, Jackie's story is quite common in the business world. While managers and business leaders may have good intentions, broken promises and disappointing work experiences cause high turnover. Workers, especially younger generations, expect guidance, coaching, and development to hone their skills. They also want a sense of purpose in their jobs and to be working for something greater than the company's bottom line. It's hard for employees to be truly connected to their organizations when this isn't the case. Though hiring managers and executives say the development of employees is a priority, it often falls flat, just like Jackie experienced. Many leaders intend to live up to these promises and ensure employees are getting appropriate training and direction, but everyone is so busy and distracted, things can easily fall by the wayside. No one ends up taking the time to actually follow up and follow through. Managers assume workers will just go off and learn to do their jobs. But without the proper mentorship, training, and attention, the whole process falls short.

We have to keep our people as the focus of everything we do! Our employees are our most valuable assets. If we want to attract and keep them, we have to prioritize their needs, their growth, and their development over everything else. Many executives jump to invest in new technologies but don't see the ROI of investing in their employees—their *human capital.*

In 2018, John Deere, a world leader in tractors, lawnmowers, agricultural equipment, and the like, was rated as more innovative than companies such as Google and Facebook. John Deere is committed to delivering cutting-edge technology that provides actionable data and produces efficiency to accelerate farming capabilities. It is constantly working to ensure every inch of farmland is productive and that farmers are able to do more with less. The company understands that as the world's population increases, the world's food and infrastructure needs will increase as well, but there will be less land, water, and natural resources available. As such, it works to manufacture high-tech engines that produce cleaner air emissions than the air going in; build products that are lighter weight, resulting in less soil compaction and reduced runoff; and provide innovative programming to educate smaller farmers across the world to promote their agricultural success. That's the reason John Deere also earned the number one ranking in the area of social innovation—work that primarily benefits society rather than specific individuals or organizations—putting it ahead of Toyota, Ford, USAA, and Honda.

Clearly John Deere's tech advancement is a huge priority! But the company also has a compelling higher purpose—to improve living standards for everyone. People are the priority for John Deere. While the company has an outstanding compensation and benefits program, prioritizes employee growth through education and career advancement, and regularly recognizes employees for their hard work, it is the focus on improving the lives of others that provides true purpose and fulfillment to their employees. John Deere even provides employees paid time off to volunteer and give back to their communities in meaningful ways. Yes, technology and innovation are crucial, but John Deere centers everything it does around inspiring its people to do more for others.[5] The takeaway here is that if we want to advance our companies, we've got to put our people first and invest in their skills, training, education, and passion just as much as we do in technology!

While some may think the "tech over humans" concept is the way of the future, research suggests that human talent is the key factor linking innovation, competitiveness, and growth in the twenty-first century.[6] Klaus Schwab, founder and executive chairman of the World Economic Forum, says, "Work shouldn't be a race between humans and machines, but a part of life that helps people recognize their full potential."[7] Experts suggest that human talent will become more valuable as technology grows because humans can brainstorm new ideas, inspire others, and drive organizations to succeed—technology cannot.[8]

Korn Ferry, a global organizational consulting firm, conducted a study that found two reasons why people outperform even the most sophisticated technology: potential and appreciation. "An individual's potential is not fixed—it can be influenced, enhanced and unleashed to benefit the organization. As people grow in knowledge, experience and seniority over time, they bring even more value to the business. In contrast, machines typically operate at a limited maximum output and depreciate over time."[9]

The only way organizations will thrive today and in the future is by creating work cultures where employees are focused on, paid attention to, and cared for, regardless of whether they work inside the company or remotely. Millennials and Gen Z see the workplace differently and want more from their jobs than just paychecks. They want more positive day-to-day work experiences, the flexibility to work from home, and the opportunity to work for companies where they aren't just numbers but where they can make a meaningful contribution. We have to accept this and find ways to use technology to create or enhance People First in our organizations in order to provide the kind of culture younger generations are seeking.

Millennials are the most disengaged generation and consequently change jobs three times more often than older generations. Numerous studies confirm that employee retention and turnover have been one of the biggest challenges for businesses, with turnover costing up to 30 percent of the position's total salary.[10] Fifty-three percent of employees say they give the minimum effort required in their jobs, so it is no wonder that actively disengaged employees cost the US $483 to $605 billion per year in lost productivity![11] At the end of the day, we need to care about our employees and mentor our people, regardless of what generation they are in, but we also need to go about it in a way that acknowledges and responds to what is important to them.

Technological advancement has complicated our ability to engage in our work. As a society, we are more connected via the internet, yet we are more disconnected *from each other* than ever before. There is a direct correlation between time spent on the internet and the level of loneliness one experiences. A 2019 Cigna survey reported that 61 percent of Americans over the age of eighteen are lonely, which is an increase from its 2018 study.[12] Technological connection is predominant, but true human connection is drastically missing from our lives. People would rather text than talk, email than converse. Instead of striking up a conversation with a coworker at lunch, we put headphones on and bury ourselves in our phones to avoid each other. A recent Harvard study found that open floor plans actually kill productivity. It decreases face-to-face time by nearly 70 percent and increases email use by up to 50 percent! Let's face it—we've created work environments that are cold, detached, and insincere.

So how do we create organizations that people want to work for? How do we inspire a younger generation of workers? How do we create thriving teams, especially when people are working remotely more often? The answer lies in humanizing our businesses and prioritizing our people.

Keeping connection at the heart of every aspect of the employee life cycle will create what we call a culture of L.O.V.E. What is L.O.V.E.? It's the Loyalty, Ownership, Value, and Excellence that permeates the organization when management invests time and energy in its people, which leads to a symbiotic employer-employee relationship. L.O.V.E. naturally occurs when business leaders make it crystal clear that their people are their most important asset and that helping them learn, grow, and evolve is of the utmost priority. In this type of environment, the flow of information and knowledge is strengthened and leads to genuine and lasting connection. Positive workplaces are created, employers become more *credible* in the eyes of job seekers, and interviews become *candid* conversations instead of intimidating interrogations.

When all of the above is in place, we begin to change the fabric of our organization. Loyalty develops in our people when we first show loyalty as employers—by *cultivating* and paying attention to them, it ensures they are fully prepared for their new role. Regularly connecting with employees beyond their first few months on the job demonstrates our *commitment* to their well-being, and in return, we begin to see them take ownership of their roles. *Caring* about employee successes, failures, and overall development produces long-term value in each individual and ultimately leads to an organization operating with excellence. In this kind of environment, workers are constantly engaging, connecting, sharing, and caring about each other, their work, and the company.

We call Credibility, Candor, Cultivation, Commitment, and Care the five steps to Pure Human Connection in the workplace, and together they create a culture of L.O.V.E. When a culture of L.O.V.E. exists, it leads to an organization that functions at a higher level. It creates a win-win scenario where employees are fulfilled and happy; and as a result, the company as a whole is flourishing.

PEOPLE FIRST

We've spent our entire careers engaging our teams, but with challenges catching and keeping people's attention, we've had to directly focus on creating a culture of L.O.V.E. When one of our best employees, Jodie, unexpectedly lost her mother two days before our biggest, most labor-intensive event of the year, we cringed. Even though Jodie vowed to still work the event, we told her to take all the time she needed to be with her family. In all honesty, it was a huge blow not to have Jodie for the event, but we knew it was in *her* best interest to not be at work, and we survived. When Casey, an assistant manager that we spent years developing, told me he was applying for his dream job at Disney, my heart sank. Casey was one of our top employees who we hoped to keep around for several more years. But we helped him fine-tune his résumé, prepped him for his interview, and provided a great reference, because that was best for Casey. Putting your people first isn't always easy, but it is always prioritizing what is best for them, not you. It means you treat your people better, and it matters.

A few years ago, Bob Chapman, CEO of manufacturing company Barry-Wehmiller, wrote a book about his Truly Human Leadership Philosophy where everybody matters. People spend most of their waking time in the office and are very frustrated by the way they are treated week in and week out. "Everyone wants to know that who they are and what they do matters," Chapman explained.[13] "We found out that how we treat people in our care materially affects how they act towards their spouses and children." Taking care of employees significantly impacts how they will treat others—their families, coworkers, customers, and community members. According to a recent article in *Forbes*, "Treating people as valuable members of the company instead of as interchangeable parts can bring about better results."[14]

It is an expectation that people will be treated better in today's world. Society is significantly less willing to accept the exploitation of others. Employees want to work for companies they can be proud of and trust to do the right thing. A few years ago, Target embarked on a sensible source initiative and made it a standard business practice to no longer buy products from factories or businesses where workers were abused or mistreated. Target has an entire division whose mission is to monitor compliance and regulation of factories and facilities supplying products to the retail chain, to ensure specific requirements are being consistently met. Child labor, poor working conditions, and excessive work hours (more than sixty/week) are unacceptable, and Target will not purchase goods from suppliers that do not comply. The company is sensitive and empathetic, as it invests tremendous resources in ensuring its people (and those of its suppliers) are treated properly. Target demonstrates what it means to be a true People First organization, because when you have a 360 degree commitment to your people, it guides every decision you make.

In 1988, Kaye Lani Rae Rafko was the first registered nurse to be crowned Miss America. In a recent interview with Jackie, she shared that as a nurse she knew the importance of seeing patients as people first, and it always bothered her that patients were defined as room numbers and illnesses. Patients would be referenced as "48-year-old male with leukemia in 31B" and Kaye Lani found herself thinking, "Why aren't we using their names?! We are *people* caring for *people*!" During her time as Miss America and to this day, Kaye Lani uses stories about her ability to connect with patients to inspire others. She often tells the story of a young patient she cared for as a nurse. He had a dream of going to Hawaii, but between his disease and the medical expenses, it was not possible. After he learned his prognosis had worsened, Kaye Lani went to his room dressed in a hula outfit, blared Hawaiian music, and danced a Polynesian dance, which was her talent when she was Miss America. It was truly a special moment that his family treasured long after their son passed away.

Sometimes we forget the impact we can have on others when we prioritize what really matters. We can easily fall into what Kaye Lani refers to as the "deep ditch" of checking things off the list and forget the reason we chose our professions in the first place. Kaye Lani has found that many doctors and nurses chose their profession simply to care for or help people. She reminds them of the importance of putting people first and urges them to see the patient first, not just the diseases or injuries. She said, "I'll never forget a patient telling me 'I remember all of my nurses.' When you think about the imprint you are leaving on a person's life, it puts things in perspective, doesn't it?"

We have the power to treat people better and the responsibility to genuinely care for those we work with each day. We all begin our careers with a sense of purpose and passion, but too often it's extinguished by the day-to-day busyness. Yet our organizations can be focused on purpose in a way that ignites employees' passion and perspective. We need to be the kind of leaders who reinforce that sense of purpose and reengage with our people so they don't become jaded and leave. Let's keep our eyes on what is right in front of us to not lose the perspective and connection to what got us there in the first place.

THE POWER OF KNOWLEDGE

In a distracted world, sometimes a little perspective brings things back into focus. When people have knowledge behind the information in front of them, they can make better decisions. They act more confidently, speak more appropriately, and are more understanding of others. With knowledge, people are able to become better versions of themselves. It can fuel passion and ignite purpose. Knowledge is a crucial component to every step you'll read about in this book, because we believe it is the foundation for connection. We define knowledge as expertise, insight, information, or awareness that is shared in a selfless way with the intention of enlightening or providing clarity to another person. It comes in many forms—wisdom, experience, stories, information, or training. Distributing knowledge is critical for organizational success because it presents clarity and perspective.

Employees gain a different perspective when they understand a company's past. When they can see where the company has been, it provides a road map for the future. Nike, the global athletic merchandising empire, has seen its fair share of ups and downs in recent years. From issues with Zion Williamson's shoe ripping during one of the biggest and most watched basketball games of the year to the Colin Kaepernick ad about kneeling during the national anthem at an NFL game, Nike is no stranger to criticism. The company has survived setbacks and weathered controversy by sticking to its company values and making a point to share its deep heritage with employees.

At Nike, many veteran executives spend time telling stories to help employees understand the company's sense of identity. To foster a deeper understanding, the company launched a corporate storytelling program where designated employees are responsible for regularly telling stories to everyone, from vice presidents to sales reps to hourly workers who run the cash registers at Nike stores. These stories are not about sales numbers or financial goals but about people living the company values, achieving something important, or overcoming a significant obstacle.

For example, Bill Bowerman, who was the track and field coach of well-known Nike cofounder Phil Knight, thought his team needed better running shoes that would perform well on any kind of surface. One morning over breakfast with his wife, Bowerman looked down at his waffles and had an idea. He jumped up from the table, went to his workshop, and poured rubber into the family waffle iron to test his theory. His innovation and quest for better sports equipment led to his creation of Nike's famous waffle-sole shoes that debuted in 1974. A version of them is still in production today.

Stories like this demonstrate the company values of performance and innovation for employees to understand, embrace, and proudly share with others. "Every company has a story," said Dave Pearson, a Nike training manager and storyteller in a *Fast Company* article. "But we have a little bit more than history. We have a heritage, something that's still relevant today. If we connect people to that, chances are they won't view Nike as just another place to work."[15]

Stories are a unique form of knowledge that provide a point of reference for employees and guide their actions and decision making. Think about how important it is for an employee's understanding to share who you are as a company during recruitment or describing your company culture in the hiring process. Sharing knowledge throughout an employee's tenure, such as giving and receiving feedback, is vital to success in any position. When it is absent, it results in employees feeling disconnected, unsupported, and disengaged.

BACK TO THE FUTURE

Do you remember apprenticeships? When I hear the word, I always picture an old-time blacksmith melting iron and handcrafting tools on an anvil as an understudy eagerly watches. Apprenticeship is a form of job training where a master of the trade takes another under his wing to share the ins and outs of his profession. In olden days, blacksmithing was a highly respected profession because villages often couldn't survive without the swords, plowshares, cooking utensils, knives, and horseshoes made by the blacksmith. The only way to pass along this unique and important craft was for an apprentice to meticulously follow and study the blacksmith. It was a process that both the master and apprentice took very seriously; after all, the master was leaving the legacy of his occupation (and likely, his life) to the next generation, and the apprentice was learning his new life's work. The master and his apprentice developed a sacred bond where knowledge was carefully shared, and the student's behaviors were lovingly guided. The master spent endless hours proudly dispensing his expertise, because the success of the apprentice was of the utmost priority. After all, if he failed, the master's legacy would die with him and the fortunes of the entire village could likely suffer.

Why don't we take teaching our people as seriously as masters once did? Why don't we revive those nurturing learning experiences that tenderly share knowledge from coworker to coworker? Today there's not a serious commitment to cultivating new or existing employees. They are thrown into a job with minimal training and ongoing development. Then, we often don't pay attention to them or give them the support they need, even though we plan to do so. During an apprenticeship, a person sat at the foot of someone else, listening and learning. It was an honor for the master to willingly profess everything he knew. Why don't we teach and encourage our experienced employees who have so much knowledge about the company, the systems, and the processes to impart their wisdom and to help other employees who are coming up in the organization? Why isn't learning and information sharing a constant in our day-to-day operation? Fifty years ago, people worked at companies for their whole lives. Think of the knowledge they had! At those times, there was continuity in passing the torch, because people took pride in articulating their expertise, and new employees were serious about learning from their valuable experience. With five generations of workers in the workforce today, there is a plethora of information to be shared! When we slow down and take the time to teach each other, our people and our organizations benefit exponentially.

When Chip Conley was invited to join the team at Airbnb at the age of fifty-two, thirty-one-year-old CEO Brian Chesky asked him to be his mentor. Both agreed it was an unusual relationship, as Conley, an experienced hotelier, says he was both a mentor *and* an intern. They learned from each other; he taught Chesky emotional intelligence, leadership skills, and strategic thinking, and Chesky taught him digital intelligence. Conley says workplaces should be "intergenerational potlucks, where people bring what they know best."[16] Companies can create a current version of the master and apprentice scenario, where coworkers on all levels share their wisdom with each other to ensure crucial company knowledge is not lost and to keep employees constantly learning.

Duke Energy, the largest regulated utility in the country, has established several initiatives to preserve valuable industry information gained from experienced employees. The goal is to ensure younger workers soak up crucial company knowledge that older ones have learned during their

PEOPLE F1RST

tenure. Duke Energy keeps knowledge front and center by asking managers to create knowledge-transfer plans for their team members reaching retirement. The plans include everything from shooting videos to job shadowing and walking young workers through complex procedures. The company even created a Monopoly-like game to teach the impact of fuel, taxes, costs, and other factors in electricity generation, giving younger workers a CEO's view of the business and unique insight into understanding the industry. Duke Energy pairs longtime employees with newcomers as part of a mentorship program to help new employees learn little nuances that might not come up in their training.[17] The company makes sure inexperienced employees are able to spend time with experienced workers to absorb all they can by connecting with these valuable resources.

PURE HUMAN CONNECTION

Connection is defined as an authentic series of moments with another human being. Think about it: when we connect with another person, it's because we hear their story, see his or her perspective, share a common experience, or have similar feelings. Bestselling author Brené Brown says, "I define connection as the energy that exists between people when they feel seen, heard and valued; when they can give and receive without judgment and when they derive sustenance and strength from the relationship."[18]

We believe that in its purest form, connection between two people happens when they are completely focused on one another. It requires intention because you must shut out all the distractions and noise around you to truly see and hear the other person. When you have intention, you are giving a little piece of yourself to the other person. We call this Pure Human Connection, and it is the foundation for Credibility, Candor, Cultivation, Commitment, and Care. Today, we are often too busy to have the intention to connect, but if we take the time to stop and focus, the most powerful connections take place.

Our favorite example of Pure Human Connection is arguably one of the greatest traditions in college football. The University of Iowa Stead Family Children's Hospital was built right next to the football stadium, and every game day, the sick children and their families gather on the top floor to watch the game through the floor-to-ceiling windows. At the end of the first quarter of each home game, the nearly seventy thousand people in the stadium shift their focus from the football field to the children's hospital, and every single person looks up and waves. The players, the coaches, the cheerleaders, the referees, and the fans wave, and not just the Hawkeyes but the opposing team too. For a few moments, the game becomes irrelevant and seventy thousand people say, "We see you. We are with you."

And it matters.

It matters to the people waving, and more importantly, it matters to those in the hospital. The impact it has on the kids who are fighting for their lives and their families who are fighting with them is indescribable and very special. In interview after interview, young patients boast that game day is their favorite day because they feel a little more normal and as if they are actually part of the game. It gives them strength and encouragement beyond measure. I recall one interview that brought us to tears watching one mom tell the camera, "For just a few minutes we aren't alone here. It means the world to us."

What does this story have to do with your company? Everything. There is real intention behind The Wave, as it's known at the University of Iowa and around the globe. It costs absolutely nothing and requires very little effort to perform, and yet it has left a lasting footprint on the hearts of hundreds of thousands of patients, players, and fans over the years. It is authentic human connection in its purest form, because for just a few minutes, the game and all the other stadium distractions stop. For moments almost frozen in time, the focus has nothing to do with football and everything to do with real people who have real problems.

Look at the power that can exist when people inside your organization have the intention to genuinely see each other and to willingly help one another. Look at the impact you can have on your team when you put aside the distractions, take a timeout from the tasks, and connect with a coworker who is in need of your attention. This is what a culture of L.O.V.E. is all about! It just takes a little time, attention, and the right intention. It can be a smile, a glance, a hug, a handshake, or a conversation. It can even be just offering a listening ear. Pure human connection is not complicated! Let's go back to times where we engaged each other in conversation in the workplace. Let's take off our headphones and step out from behind our screens and actually walk to a coworker's desk to ask a question. Let's put our phones away and look each other in the eyes. It's simplistic, yet profound, just like The Wave.

When we have the intent to connect in the workplace, we can build trust, understanding, and relationships with those with whom we work. We can connect by sharing ourselves with each other, and it elevates the lives of both the giver and the receiver. Pure Human Connection is the core of every chapter ahead, and you can't have L.O.V.E. without it. When employees are less distracted and more engaged, they stay! When a company cares more about building up employees than just building up profits, turnover decreases and the value produced increases.

In the chapters ahead, we will dive into each of the five steps of Pure Human Connection: Credibility, Candor, Cultivation, Commitment, and Care. You will be given examples and ideas to create opportunities for Pure Human Connection within your organization, and we will walk you through creating an environment where employees love to show up every day. When you follow the steps ahead, you will quickly see the difference between an organization that is surviving and one that is thriving!

CHAPTER 3:

CREDIBILITY

"It's not about what it is…it's about what
it can become."
—The Once-ler in *The Lorax,* by Dr. Seuss

On my first day, I knew my work was cut out for me, but I had no idea how big the challenge was going to be. I was the new general manager at a prominent country club in Dallas and had been hired by the old-school, prestigious private club to bring in new energy and improve the overall member experience. I expected some changes would be necessary; what I didn't anticipate was the need for a complete overhaul of club operations. It was a more dysfunctional work culture than I had ever imagined. Employees wouldn't look me in the eye, and nearly every staff person walked with their heads down, trying to be unnoticed. There was no such thing as teamwork or collaboration; it was a group of individuals working in open isolation.

After a few very frustrating days on the job, I was actually tempted to replace the entire staff because I thought it would be easier to just start over and build my team from scratch. But I quickly realized I couldn't possibly recruit the kind of rock stars I needed. The club had done a terrible job of marketing itself as an employer to the job-seeking community. The public barely knew we existed, much less what we had to offer! We had to start building our employer reputation outwardly before I could think of hiring new faces. Credibility had to be established first with our current employees if I was ever going to turn things around.

I couldn't go around telling everyone that the club in Dallas was a great place to work when our own people didn't agree. Employees were siloed, unhappy, and underappreciated. They were starved for leadership and thirsting for connection. They had never been put first and didn't even know that was possible. So the massive undertaking of transitioning WHO we were as a company began by making our people our number one priority.

Our core group of five managers led the charge. We began by *seeing* our employees as individuals and began treating them like *people* with feelings and voices. Our goal was to understand and to see things from their perspective, so we asked what we could do to make their jobs easier. We listened intently to their answers and then implemented their ideas. I was downright shocked when one employee told me, "I've worked at this club for twenty-three years, and no one has ever asked me what I thought." We showed our employees we cared about them when we took genuine interest in what they had to say—their ideas and opinions. Conversations led to connections, and connections led to genuine relationships. When we did what we said we would do and we practiced what we preached, we proved we were dependable. It didn't happen overnight, but once we shared the story of what we were trying to achieve, our employees understood the vision and their role in fulfilling it. Sharing this kind of information was critical in establishing our credibility because it gave employees a lens to look through to see who we were becoming as an organization. It didn't take long for our people to begin coming to work excited and eager to offer ideas and solutions. We soon noticed they were beginning to work together, helping one another and enjoying their jobs more.

As an organization, your credibility is how you are seen in the world, whether it's internally by employees or externally by job seekers. It represents WHO you are as a company, and that knowledge is shared outwardly to the public. In today's highly digital era, the ability to access information about a company's true culture on job review sites means you can't hide anything! Truth and transparency have never been more crucial as they are today. For example, if you claim to have a diverse and inclusive company, you better be practicing what you preach, or you'll be called out and scrutinized on social media! To be credible in the eyes of the public, you must have a genuine and consistent message that is focused on putting your People First. Credibility is the first step to Pure Human Connection because it is the initial point of contact with the world. It represents your culture, how you treat your employees, and whether you are truly living your mission, purpose, and values. A lack of transparency or truthfulness can be crushing to your Credibility, and it can sink an organization or one of its leaders. But when you are seen as Credible, you are recognized as a trustworthy and reliable employer. Your Credibility is extremely important. It is the crux of your company, and it matters more than anything else you do.

GETTING IT RIGHT

"Employer brand" is a huge buzzword these days because businesses everywhere are realizing that you have to have an authentic message that communicates an employee-centric culture with a clear mission, defined purpose, and strong values. In our case, our Credibility was strengthened by creating a culture of integrity and by putting our people first. When you prioritize your people, you create a win-win scenario for your organization. Your employees win because they feel valued and empowered; they are all in and want to contribute to the company goals and its ultimate success. They also become your ambassadors, spreading an overall positive picture outside the walls of your company. Not only are employees recruiting potential employees and possible customers for you, they are also loyal, committed, and engaged! This leads to lasting employee value, a thriving operation, and a win for your company.

We recognize we are living in a customer-driven world where too many companies are focused on the end product—the customer. But if you don't focus on your employees first, you won't be able to impact the entire result! That was where the club in Dallas was missing the mark. For years, the club prioritized its members over everything else, employees included. Ultimately it became the primary cause of poor member service and a lacking environment.

Chick-fil-A is a classic example of a People First organization. Every Sunday, all of its thousands of restaurants close so employees can enjoy a day of rest and worship. The company could bring in millions more dollars each year by opening on Sundays, yet it doesn't. Chick-fil-A is true to its founding principles and values employees more than profits. That speaks volumes about its Credibility.

The unfortunate reality is that too many companies have false Credibility. They say they are a People First environment or they put out a powerful message, but they don't practice what they preach. Red Ventures, a marketing and advertising firm, received several positive reviews on Glassdoor due to great perks such as an indoor basketball court, great benefits, and super-smart coworkers. But the company also received numerous negative reviews citing an impossible work/life balance, lack of diversity in senior executives, a vague company direction, and not holding true to what was promised during interviews. We see this as an example of faltering Credibility and believe it was the reason the company experienced high turnover.

Not practicing what you preach or not following through on promises is a major turnoff, and it drives good people away.[19] That is why we had to start inside our own four walls at the club in Dallas before we could begin recruiting outside. The next generation of workers is looking for more than just a paycheck—it is inspired by jobs where the work is meaningful and seeks employers who are truthful. Today's workforce wants to be part of a bigger community working together to achieve something great. So in order to keep quality workers, you have to do what you say you are going to do and be who you say you are. You can't fake the People First philosophy!

Some companies are getting it right with their Credibility and are firing on all cylinders. Everyone talks about Google as a great place to work; 91 percent of its employees recommend it as an employer. Known for its out-of-the-box work environment and unique employee benefits, Google allows employees to select the projects of most interest to them and gives them access to outdoor sports parks, volleyball courts, rock climbing walls, gyms, massages, and even music lessons. The thing that underlies all their unusual perks is that the organization is really focused on employee wellness, happiness, and energy. Google recognizes that employee innovation is at its peak when employees are happy and fulfilled.

Starbucks touts diversity, growth, and community involvement. Offering great benefits, partnership, and investment opportunities for employees, Starbucks speaks to people's desire to be connected to a community of family and friends.

Salesforce, a customer relationship management (CRM) platform, welcomes employees into their Ohana, the Hawaiian word for family. Truly living out its commitment to transparency, the company website takes interested candidates through a step-by-step overview of the hiring process so applicants know exactly what to expect. Employee happiness and well-being are the foundation for every business decision the company makes.

Google, Starbucks, and Salesforce are three better-known examples of very successful companies that have mastered sharing their story with the outside world in a way that resonates with and attracts talented, high-quality employees who *want* to contribute to the organization's goals. Constantly educating the job-seeker community on the benefits of being an employee and the perks of their company cultures through their websites, internet videos, and social media sites, Google, Starbucks, and Salesforce understand that employer reputation is the linchpin in an organization's success. It is so crucial that 69 percent of candidates say they would *not* take a job with a company that had a bad reputation, even if they were unemployed.[20]

Mastering your Credibility is essential for finding the right kind of people for your team. You want to connect with candidates who encompass beliefs similar to your organization, people who share the same values, understand your mission, and feel drawn to your company purpose. Sixty-nine percent of candidates are likely to apply for a job if the employer actively manages its employer brand, and 76 percent want details on what makes the company an attractive place to work, according to Glassdoor research.[21] That's why you must clearly establish the message of WHO you are as a company and then tie that message to everything that you do.

USING MVPS TO ATTRACT MVPS

When I first came in to the club in Dallas, I knew we had to overhaul the culture completely if we were going to affect radical change. To do that, we first had to establish the Mission, Vision, and Purpose of our organization in order to transform ourselves and our company as a whole. We call this our MVP program, and it creates clarity, unity, and direction within the organization, which ultimately leads to having a team of MVPs (most valuable players). Our MVP program is the launchpad for building lasting Credibility because it intrinsically changes the organization.

For us, the club was so broken foundationally that we started with our Purpose instead of our Mission. We couldn't begin crafting our Mission when our team didn't even understand our WHY. We put all of our management staff and key department heads in a room off-site for a two-day retreat so we could engage in uninterrupted discussions to uncover our MVP. When I asked the group what our purpose was, I got a lot of blank stares and mutters of "to take care of the members." "Why does our club exist? Why are we doing what we do?" I asked. The entire group was surprised by how long it took us to figure this out. We kept digging by asking "Why?" every time an answer was thrown out to the group. We finally determined that our country club's purpose was to be a place of refuge for our members and their families. Carefully crafting our newfound purpose into a message that was inspiring to our team, we wrote: "First-class people delivering world-class service while creating lifelong memories for our members." Our team was proud to be classified as first class and was motivated to provide outstanding service, but the crux of our purpose was to create experiences for our members that they would always remember—Mother's Day Brunch with their family, the Fourth of July under the fireworks, their children meeting Santa Claus for the first time, and so on.

What is your WHY? Finding your purpose comes from answering this question. It is intended to engage and inspire employees—to drive their performance. Bring your team together and rid yourselves of all the normal day-to-day distractions. Spend time digging into your WHY and reveal your true purpose as an organization, ignite your team, and unleash their motivation.

When we moved on to identify our Mission, things got a little more heated. Our management team of eighteen was challenged when we dove deep into understanding what we do and how it connected to our WHY. We found that half of us thought our focus was on the end result—our members—and the other half of us thought the focus was on our team—our employees. Those who had been part of the "old regime" were having a hard time placing priority on our people—our employees—over our customers—our members.

After hours of intense debate and discussion, we revealed a Mission that highlighted our cultural transformation from a subservient environment to a take-charge, friendly, and collaborative workplace. We wrote: "As a team, we will lead the membership to the premiere experience, and we are happy to do it." Our Mission spoke to our servant leadership mentality and our ability to function as one team, and it ensured that we would always strive for excellence. For us, understanding what it was that we were there to do every day had been muddled and confusing. When we hammered out our Mission statement—what the company does and what it is known for—a healthy debate took place. WHAT were we going to do? Lead! And be happy while doing it! We were surprised how our passion was resurrected when we connected our WHY with our WHAT. It was energizing—as though we had emerged from a dark tunnel into sunlight!

The next day when we returned to our secluded spot to identify our core values, they quickly bubbled to the surface. Values are your belief system and will be the compass that directs HOW your people will behave. When our team talked about HOW we wanted our employees to act now and in the future, everyone weighed in with their recommendations. Those who had worked for the club for many years were outspoken—they had experienced a toxic work environment and were ready for positive change. Trust, honor, pride, dedication, discipline, persistence, transparency, optimism, professionalism, and loyalty were just a few on our very long list of values deemed important in building our new culture. Each person contributed at least one idea so it was a true collective effort. We then began to narrow those values into a more manageable few. Categorizing similar words and definitions into groups, we selected the best possible word for each category and came up with integrity, respect, accountability, leadership, and fun-loving spirit. We all agreed these five values described us perfectly, and they encapsulated everything we stood for and everything we needed to be in order to achieve our mission and purpose. When you set the values and get buy-in from your team, you create an environment where your people live and breathe that belief system.

When we finally had our MVP all laid out, we were able to see the company in a whole new light. We went from juggling day-to-day duties to leading our club in a strategic and confident manner. Instead of being consumed by putting out little fires, our fresh perspective gave us the motivation to set our new reality into motion. We began planning an event for our members that would blow their minds and give them an experience they had never had. We called it a "block party"—the visual representation of the transformation we were going through as a club. We were going to enthusiastically lead our members to a premiere experience...and we did! We'll tell you the whole story in the chapters to come.

What could this MVP program look like for you? Take a look at your company purpose. Is it inspiring? How can you transform the message in a way that excites and influences your employees to give their best efforts? Does your mission statement feel generic? Is it too much about a product or too focused on the bottom line? What are the values by which your company operates? Are they relevant, motivating, and easy to understand? When you can create a distinct mission and purpose and identify your core values, it is clear to everyone in the company what their roles are as individuals, team members, and as an organization. When employees know their purpose, role, mission, and the values by which they should operate, they are inspired to produce results.

Businesses that have a solid MVP and communicate it with clarity become very attractive to job seekers. For example, Kickstarter, a fund-raising platform available to the masses, has a simple yet empowering mission: *our mission is to help bring creative projects to life*. The company believes that art and creative expression is essential to a vibrant community and puts the power in the hands of the creative people by connecting them to their communities. Kickstarter is a for-profit organization that "prioritizes positive outcomes for society as much as our shareholders." Its website boasts, "Our corporate charter also lays out specific goals and commitments to put our values into our operations, promote arts and culture, fight inequality and help creative projects happen.[22] Compelling? Inspiring? Absolutely!

Once you have honed your MVP, you can craft your story and begin outwardly sharing it with the world. A few years ago, Jackie and I saw a brilliant GE commercial that left us speechless. It started with a dreamlike fantasy where the moon sinks into the sea as a young girl says, "My mom makes underwater fans that are powered by the moon." She continues, "My mom makes airplane engines that can talk," as airplanes with feather wings take to the sky. The commercial ended with the little girl looking straight into the camera and proudly boasting, "My mom works at GE." We both stared at the TV, mouths open, completely mesmerized. Here was this huge company spending millions of dollars on a commercial that was not trying to sell a product but rather to make a statement about why they are a great place to work! I have no engineering capabilities whatsoever, but after watching that commercial, I wanted to work for GE! The company communicated in a powerful, genuine way that its mission is to provide innovative technology that will build, move, power, and cure the world. GE's purpose was clear and went beyond the surface level to state that it doesn't just want to innovate; it wants people to be positively impacted by its technologies. This spoke to who it was as an organization. This ad told a story that said you can be proud of what you do and you can make a difference in the lives of others when you work at GE.

When it came to sharing our story at the club in Dallas, we did it with excitement and authenticity. We had to reinforce our Credibility and reignite our people's passion at the same time so we told anyone who would listen—members, vendors, community leaders, job seekers, and employees—our plan to transform the outdated private club into a cool, energetic, family-centric resort where fun was the focus for everyone—members *and* employees. In every interview we conducted, we shared the story of where we were going—Jackie even included a hand gesture to visually represent our journey. Her hand would start at chest level, parallel to the floor, to show where we had been; then her hand raised to chin level to show where we were currently; and then her hand went as high up as it could go to show where we were going. It might sound silly, but it was simple and clear. Sometimes communicating without using words can be powerful! Our energy and genuine enthusiasm were contagious, and our story quickly became legendary in the community.

Sharing your MVP is essential for attracting and Cultivating workers who are passionate about your success, and it is the key to sparking a connection with current and future employees to generate buy-in. Get ready for your entire organization to transcend and your culture to shift as employees embrace your WHY, WHAT, and HOW.

CREATING A CULTURE CLUB

Several years ago Levi Strauss, the world-renowned jeans giant, took on the initiative to reinvent their Credibility. The program, called the "Worker Well-being initiative," was designed to enhance the lives of workers while also amplifying business results. Levi Strauss wanted to transform the culture in its factories by "recognizing that workers aren't faceless cogs in a giant profit machine, but people with feelings and needs."[23] The goal was to create more productive and better-run factories with happier, healthier employees, which would ultimately lead to lower costs and better profits. Levi Strauss realized that the only way to drastically improve the company's value was to put its people first!

Before this initiative, employees were afraid to speak up. Communication was one-sided from management, and employees weren't treated particularly well. Basically, employees worked there because they needed a job, not because they wanted to.

When Levi Strauss committed to focusing on its people, it began by improving the physical environment. Previously overlooked necessities like cold water from new water fountains and cooler air from new overhead fans were installed in the factories. By recognizing basic needs, Levi Strauss set a foundation for trust that they could then build upon. The next step was training supervisors to be kinder and more communicative to all subordinates. By focusing on gender equality and inclusiveness, supervisors began regularly asking for input, opinions, and expertise from line-level workers, and employees began to feel vested in the overall success of the company. Respect and transparency were the cornerstones of this dynamic cultural shift that resulted in workers who were more engaged and willing to put forth their best efforts. Months after making the transition to an employee-centric culture, Levi Strauss revealed that absenteeism was down, turnover had been reduced, and the bottom line was significantly improved. Clearly the People First focus changed the game![24]

Fostering a positive work culture—what we call a Culture Club—is critical for success in any business. People put more weight on what others *say* about a company or product than any other form of information. As previously mentioned, the internet, social media, job review sites, and word of mouth are highly effective and powerful marketing tools; but they can also "call out" employers for poor working conditions, toxic cultures, lack of diversity, discrimination, or unfair treatment of employees. When employees are miserable, overworked, underappreciated, or treated unfairly, it usually stems from a lack of interaction with management or an environment where employees are afraid to speak up or present new ideas. Workplaces like this are hazardous and can lead to a constant turnover of employees, diminished productivity, and a struggle to find quality candidates for open positions. In today's transparent online-driven world, if your current and former employees aren't engaged or happy, they are likely to be talking negatively about your company and putting your Credibility at risk.

Like Levi Strauss, we had to go back to the basics to build trust with our team at the club in Dallas. We gathered feedback from employees and immediately improved working conditions by repainting the employee cafeteria and installing TVs. Outdated, uncomfortable uniforms and old-fashioned employee policies were upgraded. Knowledge sharing was encouraged by conducting team huddles during each shift and having regular interactive management team meetings to spark camaraderie. Inclusion became a priority, and we began infusing diversity into the 95 percent Hispanic staff by hiring people of all genders, races, and ethnic backgrounds. We took things to another level by making a conscious effort to connect with employees on a daily basis. We learned about their families and what was happening in their lives. By focusing on our culture in this way, we had happier, more fulfilled employees. It boosted employee morale, strengthened the ability to attract higher-level candidates, and elevated our Credibility overall.

To create a Culture Club at your business, you have to make your people the priority and live it 100 percent. The way you treat your employees should be the way you treat your customers and the people who provide services to you! Think about how many people who are not employees yet are involved in helping your business be successful: the UPS driver, delivery people for your vendors, insurance representatives, electricians, window washers, and so on. How often do you stop from your everyday craziness to learn their names or introduce yourself? The truth is if they don't know you, they don't really care about you, and they certainly aren't going the extra mile to get your company everything it needs.

We saw this with Jeff, our mailman at the club in Dallas. He had delivered mail to our club for years, but he was usually just seen as an interruption. As we evolved our culture, we began showing *all* our people that we cared—vendors included. We got to know them, and they got to know us. Like all of our primary service providers, we invited Jeff to enjoy lunch in our employee break room if he was at the club around lunchtime. Jeff ended up planning his delivery route around having lunch at our club every day! He sat with our staff and was often laughing and telling stories. He built relationships with our employees and felt such a part of our team that he wanted us to be as successful as we did! When it came time for an urgent mailing to go out or if we needed a second pickup later in the day, Jeff would finish his route and come back happily to provide the extra service we needed. The old mailman creed accurately described Jeff: "Neither snow nor rain nor heat nor gloom of night" could stop him from meeting our needs. Over the years, he told hundreds of people about our club, how much he loved what we were about and what a great place it was to work. We had dozens of potential employees apply for jobs because the *mailman* had recruited them for us!

Watch your Credibility ascend to a new level when you shift from seeing vendors as those who should be grateful for *your* business to having the mindset of being grateful for *their* service. You might just be surprised at what happens!

To begin a culture revolution and elevate your Credibility, incorporate the following:

Conduct a Culture Audit

While many companies are eliminating employee surveys because they find them useless, we believe in constantly gathering feedback from employees. Finding out what is working, what isn't, and how people are feeling has to come from employees through genuine and organic conversation; otherwise you likely won't get honest feedback. Every time we embark on a new policy or initiative, I send three or four of my key managers to gather feedback on the idea. They sit with a few employees in the break room or catch a couple of people during setup and in a low-key, relaxed way ask, "Hey, what

CREDIBILITY

do you guys think about this?" Collecting feedback and finding out what's really happening with line-level employees is as simple as asking them how they feel or how things are going. Are they frustrated? Do they feel valued? Are things going well in their department? Do they see how their job is intertwined with the company at large? Then the key managers and I sit down and talk about what they learned, and they use it to make decisions. If concerns are brought up, we dig deeper and conduct more research. You don't need a formal employee survey, but it's wise to assign a key person on staff to keep a pulse on employee temperament, issues, and feelings and then report that information to management on a regular basis.

Nominate a Culture Czar

Of course the Culture Czar is going to have a real job title and other duties, but they are "appointed" to this position to safeguard the company culture and to ensure that the core elements of the MVP don't go awry in the day-to-day operations. Shortly after starting at the club in Dallas, I hired Jackie to not only be the club's assistant manager, but more importantly, to be our Culture Czar. She lived and breathed our MVP. When an employee was gossiping or causing drama, Jackie personally reminded him or her of our mission and that negativity was not part of WHO we were as an organization anymore. When a department head took out his frustrations on his department and was mistreating the employees, Jackie quickly pulled him into a room to privately make it clear that his stress could not derail all that we were working toward. When we'd had a busy week and some people were lacking energy, Jackie acted as our cheerleader and built up the team with encouragement.

The Culture Czar should be the face of the company and the culture. Find someone who oozes positivity and encouragement and also perfectly aligns with your MVP. You want the kind of person who is promoting teamwork and keeping your culture on track. If one person can't cover your entire organization, consider appointing departmental Culture Czars who report to the main one, and have them all collaborate regularly.

43

Model Your Message

It might seem simple, but it is essential: as a leader in your organization, you must model your message. If you go around promoting that your core values are trust and integrity and then employees find out that you lied to them, all of the effort to transform your culture will be erased. With us, authenticity, trust, respect, and transparency were critical to our success. If we hadn't consistently talked about this with our management team, then we likely would have found it even more difficult to build Credibility with our employees. Always be aware of department heads or key players on your team who aren't modeling your overall message, because inconsistency will defeat your employee-centric goals. Be sure your leadership team is cognizant of how its actions and behavior will impact the entire team and the company culture.

Look Outside Your Four Walls

What can you do to enhance the lives of the people in your neighborhood? Our management team volunteered six times each year to spend an afternoon with kids and parents at the Scottish Rite for Children pediatric hospital, and every one of us would tell you that we got more out of it than the kids did. You are never too busy to get out from behind your computer screen to touch those in your community. We live in a disconnected, distracted, and transactional world, and your effort to connect will far outweigh anything you do behind your desk!

When was the last time you conducted employee training or open discussion based on issues happening in society? For your team, it has to be about more than just work; they need to be fulfilled in all aspects of their lives, and their work needs to be tied to what is happening outside your four walls. Our world is more polarized than ever. Social issues, the political environment, and identity issues all impact the general public, but they seep into the workplace too. Be sensitive and aware of these issues, because you can't disconnect your company and your employees from what's going on in the world around you. If you want to transform your Credibility, be in tune with what is happening beyond the business and be sensitive to how it is impacting your team. Have conversations to connect with your employees on how they are feeling. Ask them what your organization could be doing both in your business and in the community. That is pure human connection at its finest.

ROCK STARS WANTED

As Jackie approached her second summer at Wakonda Club in Des Moines, Iowa, where we worked together before going to the club in Dallas, she was smarter, more experienced, and focused on what she wanted. She had survived the busiest months of the year during the previous summer with long hours and dozens of seasonal employees, but now she was looking at her role from the bigger picture. When she walked into my office that spring to ask me a question, I was completely caught off guard.

"Three, I want to change up our job ads," she said. So I asked her to explain what she was thinking. "You told me to evaluate last summer and what we could have done differently. You said I should hire more people like me—energetic, outgoing, hard workers. I call them 'rock stars.' But when I looked at our ads, I realized rock stars would never apply for our jobs given how we are presenting the positions to them." She paused, and I nodded in agreement. "You're right; our ads really are boring," I said as I read our current ad: WAKONDA CLUB NOW HIRING FOR FULL- AND PART-TIME SUMMER STAFF. APPLY WITHIN.

Jackie took a deep breath and clutched the paper in her hands. She gave me a nervous look as she handed me the piece of paper. It read:

R U Ready 2 Rock?!

WE R!

Join the Team at Wakonda Club Today!

I panicked. This was a drastic shift in the way we did things! And this was years ago, way before text message talk was ever seen! I didn't want this to damage our reputation in the community, but I also didn't want to squash Jackie, who had come to me with a fresh idea to improve our recruiting efforts. I contemplated for a bit but finally said, "Let's give it a shot."

I will never forget that day, as I learned an incredible lesson. That summer, Jackie hired the absolute best staff I had ever worked with. Most were college and high school kids who were full of life, highly engaged, hardworking, and just plain good people. Our members raved about the service and the energy at the club. The rest of our staff commented that work had never been so much fun. I learned how powerful the right wording could be in capturing the attention of the right people. I discovered that when you advertise jobs in an energetic and unique way, you stand out and can more readily connect with the kind of people who are drawn to your message. I also learned the importance of listening to your employees' ideas and giving them a chance to prove themselves. More on this later.

All my life, people have told me that I should be in sales. I always laugh because I hate selling and could never be a salesperson. But I realized that my way of "selling" is just by being myself—enthusiastic and authentic. When I look at it from their perspective, I guess I am selling in a way, but what I'm really doing is celebrating WHO we are as an organization and where we are going. This ultimately draws others in and they want to be part of it. People do not want to be sold or marketed to; they want to connect to it and *feel* what someone is offering so they can come to see things on their own. Don't sell your story in a slick way; be heartfelt, real, and relatable. Providing information in a casual yet confident and appealing way is what wins people over. Instead of *selling* others on your company, give them the information they need to decide whether your company is right for them. After all, you are not trying to recruit *every* one; you are trying to recruit the *right* ones. And the right ones are those who align with your MVP.

Credibility must be constantly and consistently paid attention to; in today's world, one bad thing can cause irreparable damage. The people you hire become a product of your culture, so you have to create the kind of setting where the focus is on bringing in good people who have the opportunity to flourish.

We do everything we can to keep our good people happy. Here's an example. After four different employees approached us about Vincent, we knew we had to do something. Vincent had worked at the club in Dallas for many years and was a favorite employee of countless members. A server in our most popular restaurant, he had been bullying the new servers and pressuring them to complete his daily cleanup duties and cover for him during extra breaks. This was a tricky situation, because politically, firing Vincent would have been unfavorable with our members, but keeping Vincent was cancerous to our culture. I pulled our core team together and collectively we determined that we had to get rid of him. He was setting a bad example for our new employees, and we did not want people like this in our environment. Members *and* employees were astonished at what happened. When Vincent was let go, the rest of the team thrived! We fired a longtime, experienced employee, but service improved! It turned out that he was doing more damage than he was good.

Although we want good cultures to happen to good people, the unfortunate truth is that all too often bad cultures happen to good people. A few years ago, Wells Fargo created a toxic work environment because it set such high sales goals, employees felt compelled to lie, cheat, and swindle customers just to keep their jobs.[25] Pushed to sell products beyond reason, employees were often stressed to the point of being physically ill. If sales quotas weren't achieved, staff members were pulled into a back room and threatened with the loss of their jobs. Illegal and questionable business practices became the norm, and eager, ambitious employees began leaving the company in droves to escape the pressure and negativity. This is the perfect example of a bad work culture happening to good people. Through these actions, Wells Fargo severely damaged their Credibility. Would you want to work at an organization with those kinds of values?

Companies such as SAS, an analytical software company, illustrate what happens when good culture happens to good people. Authentic, People First companies like SAS help employees see the difference they are making in the lives of others and do what they can to make work enjoyable. SAS boasts, "We eliminate unnecessary distractions and help relieve everyday stress so our employees are happier, healthier and proud of the difference their work makes." Its turnover rate is 4 percent, far below the 15 percent industry average; clearly the commitment to employee health, well-being, and work-life balance is effective.[26]

As we transformed the club in Dallas, we built a relationship with the hospitality program at a nearby university and attended their career fair to recruit interns and summer staff. It wasn't until Jackie elbowed me as I said goodbye to the student I was chatting with that I noticed what was really going on around us. Our booth had a line of twenty-five or more kids eagerly waiting to talk to us. We had five team members in our booth, and all of them were talking to students—some to two or three students at a time! As I looked around the room to the other booths, there were not more than two or three students at each one; ours was like a buzzing beehive! Students had heard from other students how great it was to work at our club; they learned what we were trying to achieve and wanted to be part of it. Our Credibility was working its magic—we had accomplished our goal! Once you are Credible in the eyes of employees and job seekers, you have the ability to hire the right kind of people with the utmost transparency and authenticity. It's what we call Candor.

CHAPTER 4:

CANDOR

"It is our choices that show what we truly are, far
more than our abilities."
—J. K. Rowling

It wasn't going well. In fact, it was painful to watch. Jackie and I were interviewing Tyler for a busboy position, and we could almost see his brain working to come up with answers he thought we wanted to hear. He was sweating and stuttering. To be fair, he was only seventeen, and we were quite intimidating in our suits. It isn't our normal practice to have the CEO and the clubhouse manager interviewing a busboy, but we'd had a string of failures in the position and needed to find the right person who could own the job. We teamed up to increase our chances of finding a rock star for the position. For fifteen minutes we had been trying to draw out something—anything—that would give us an indication of who Tyler really was. His résumé was one paragraph (he had bagged groceries for a while), and his nerves were derailing any possibility of a smooth conversation.

That's usually when you politely end the interview and thank the candidate for their interest in the open position. Tyler's stooped shoulders seemed to show that even he was waiting for us to point him toward the door. Instead of racing off to answer the unread emails in my inbox, I tried a different approach. I smiled and offhandedly asked him, "Tyler, why do you want to work at this club?" He responded to my renewed enthusiasm and didn't miss a beat. He looked out the window at the perfectly manicured lawns outlined with bright flowers and surrounded by lush green trees and smiled. "Because it's so beautiful here," he replied. His amazement and childlike innocence made Jackie chuckle. Tyler's moment of honesty revealed to us in a simple and small way that there was more to him than what we had seen thus far.

Sensing an opportunity, I leaned forward in my chair, looked him squarely in the eye, smiled, and pointed to the stack of résumés. "Tyler, why should I hire you over them?" I asked. "Why are you the best person for the job?" It wasn't a challenge or a move to provoke him. I wanted more. I wanted him to stop thinking about the answer and just speak. I needed to see something real from him. He took his time and said, "Well…my dad died a couple of months ago, and now I'm all that my mom has left. I want to work hard because I want to make my mom…and dad proud." His whole demeanor changed. He seemed comfortable for the first time, and he made eye contact with us. It felt like he had literally come clean. In that moment, we connected. He had shared his truth, his heart. Jackie and I looked at each other: we had finally found the right person.

Tyler and his interview stand out as one of our favorite experiences of connecting with a potential employee, because by all typical standards, we shouldn't have hired him. He flubbed the interview, had zero experience, and frankly, he was completely awkward. But looking past all of that, in one sentence he showed us that he had a purpose, passion, and a desire to excel as a person. We hired Tyler, who quickly became a valuable member of our team. He was hardworking, dedicated, a problem solver, and a leader in training. He stayed with us for seven years, which in the service business is very rare. Tyler made his part-time busboy job his own; he became the best busboy we had. After a few months when we promoted him to the valet department, he became our best valet. He was our "go to" guy when we needed someone to help out in other areas, and he was liked and re-spected by everyone in our organization. Looking back on that interview, we are so thankful we didn't jump to disqualify him. We were empathetic, patient, and focused. We saw Tyler as a person first and made finding the right person the priority. This made it possible for us to realize Tyler wanted to prove himself; he wanted a place to belong and just needed the chance to do so. That's why we agree with leadership expert and entrepreneur Isaac

Tolpin when he says, "I believe there are very few activities in a company as important as hiring the right person for the right job."

Many successful executives recognize that hiring is critical to the success of a business. Steve Jobs, the former CEO and cofounder of Apple Computer, believed hiring was the most important thing he did. In fact he never delegated hiring to someone else. We have always made hiring a priority in our organizations, but we take it a step further by focusing less on the formality of an interview. Instead we place the significance on connecting with WHO the candidate really is. Finding out WHO a person is requires intention, and it means you must penetrate the veneer to discover their character and core values. For us, it's about uncovering what's important to them, what their passions are, what drives and inspires them. When we were interviewing Tyler, we were focused on WHO he was from beginning to end; even when he was bombing the interview, we didn't quit on him. Instead, we pushed. We listened. We got him to open up and be vulnerable, and then—we truly connected. When you take the time to bond on a more personal level, an immediate relationship can be formed.

When a hiring process revolves around WHO people are versus what they know or what kind of work experience they have, it changes the game. It creates the opportunity to bring the right people to your team. Hiring a candidate based on a résumé, previous job title, or his or her ability to perform during an interview is unfortunately not a reliable determination of job performance. Even companies like Google haven't figured out how to effectively use interviews to determine employee performance or lasting value. Laszlo Bock, former senior vice president of people operations at Google, admitted, "We looked at tens of thousands of interviews, and [at how] everyone who had done the interviews and [how] they scored the candidate, and how that person ultimately performed in their job. We found zero relationship."[27]

FINDING WHO FITS

With many employees working remotely these days, more companies are relying on virtual interviews. This was accelerated during COVID, but the practices we discuss in this chapter apply regardless of the setting. Even though remote interviews or prerecorded videos of answers to questions can speed the process, interviewers should never lose sight of the importance of Pure Human Connection. Whether the interview is virtual or in person, focus on WHO the candidate is—it's a more efficient way to determine cultural fit, alignment with the position requirements, and ultimately whether that person will be an asset to your team. By getting rid of the old-school interview mindset where you only ask questions about experience and skills, you can start digging into WHO the people are sitting in front of you!

A few years ago, we were replacing our head golf professional at the private country club I was managing. This was an important position and one that involved a committee of members, a group of key employees, and a strategic interview process. Candidates were rated by all the employees they interacted with on whether they would fit with our team and our culture. The comments were submitted to me to be discussed with the interview committee at the end of each interview. One of the candidates was extremely qualified for the job and had a particularly impressive résumé, past experience, and references. We thought he was our guy, so we weren't surprised when he aced the interview. But much to my chagrin, the employees' impressions said otherwise—people found him to be rude, condescending, and uninterested in what others had to say. One was even candid enough to say, "He's an asshole!" Clearly his WHO had been revealed, and the employees recognized that his values did not align with ours. The committee and I immediately dismissed him from consideration.

Have you ever hired someone who interviewed flawlessly but seemed to be a completely different person after a few days on the job? A person might be able to fake their way through an interview, but that façade can't last for long. Wouldn't it be much more effective to discover WHO someone truly is when you are actually interviewing?

In our minds, the foundation for uncovering the WHO is Candor. It's an open and candid conversation that breaks through the interview "performance." Candor is the spark for initiating and building relationships. Aligning WHO your employees are with WHO your company is strengthens your chain of Credibility and reinforces the People First mindset. When you focus on the person in the chair instead of the candidate in the interview, Candor is your intention and connection is your goal.

We have hired people who were engaged, loyal, productive, and full of life. The bonds we formed as teammates were so strong that many of us are still great friends, even though we haven't worked together in years. We collaborated, supported each other, and achieved great things together. The reason we were able to create such a dynamic work culture was because we saw each employee as a person first. We created a community, a cohesive tribe that was a reflection of the beliefs and values that we share. So during our hiring process, we look for personality and attitude, not just skills and experience. We seek passion, energy, drive, and integrity. We have an open dialogue, not an intimidating interview. Imagine if all interviews shed the cloak of performance by both the interviewer and interviewee and instead became powerful, authentic conversations!

SHARE YOUR KNOWLEDGE, SHARE YOUR STORY

Shifting from a cold, formal interview process to a conversation of connection requires sharing knowledge. We invite interviewees to share their story and then we listen. Entering into an interview with the intention to share and exchange stories, or knowledge about one another, transforms the interaction from a back-and-forth question and answer session into a meaningful opportunity for something deeper. Their story may include a glimpse into their expertise or insight to their core values. It may provide clarity as to their passions, motivations, inspirations, and desires. Listening to their story reveals the kind of value they will bring to your team.

After meeting the interviewee, start the conversation with, "Tell me about yourself and what brought you here today." People tend to relax when talking about themselves and their past experiences, so this is a way to break the ice and loosen up the interviewee. An essential ingredient for Candor is a relaxed and safe environment. A person cannot be their true self when they are tense or nervous, so focusing on making the interviewee comfortable—coming at it from a place of genuine care and interest—has to be a priority. When an interviewee can't answer a question, don't just call it a red flag and dismiss the candidate so you can move on to the next. Instead, be a coach and guide them through the conversation like a guidance counselor advising a student.

Jackie once interviewed a woman who had been a stay-at-home mom for nearly fifteen years who was so nervous during the interview she could barely function. She apologized almost thirty times and kept losing her train of thought. Understanding her feelings and fears, Jackie complimented her on her bracelet and asked if the beads had any significance. The woman smiled and said it was a gift from her husband and each bead represented her three children and their favorite memories as a family. For nearly five full minutes, the conversation had nothing to do with the job, the company, or even the woman's qualifications, but it was all that mattered at that moment. Jackie got her to focus on something other than the interview and the woman calmed down, became more confident, and revealed her WHO. She was dedicated, warm, and gracious, which was exactly what Jackie was looking for in that position. It wasn't about the canned response; it was much deeper than that. It was about finding someone with a loving and nurturing disposition, and she had it. Jackie hired the woman, who was a wonderful employee for a number of years.

Having a genuine conversation requires an organic exchange of insight and experiences. Many interviewers believe that the candidate should do the majority of the talking during an interview, but we believe it should be a 50/50 split. Telling your story is important too. I often share some of my background and then delve into my leadership philosophies. When we are sharing information about ourselves, we make it a point to demonstrate vulnerability and authenticity, because that is what we want to see from the interviewee. We show our WHO to encourage the candidate to reveal his or her WHO as well.

During our time at the club in Dallas, which we discussed in the Credibility chapter, we obviously had our work cut out for us in completely rebuilding both the culture and our team at the same time. During interviews, we found that sharing our company story in a genuine and transparent way enhanced our ability to connect and added value to the conversation. Even though sharing and listening to each other's stories improves the interview, finding the right people to join your team is still difficult. Filling our roster of rock stars in Dallas did not come without its challenges.

FILL THE ROLE, NOT THE HOLE

Like most executives, we've had our share of hiring mishaps. We all dread hiring. It's a time-consuming process, and everyone is very busy. In today's digital world, it is possible for employers to receive hundreds of applicants for a single position. That is great, but it can make the process even more overwhelming. You sift through the applications and pick a handful of qualified candidates, but you still have to conduct interviews, with no guarantee you will find the right person. And if you don't, you start all over again. It can be draining and tempting to just fill the hole with an able-bodied person. But you have to ignore all of that and remember that the decision you are making is important. A hasty one can cost your organization big-time.

According to G&A Partners, a full HR service firm, the cost to replace a terminated employee is about 50 percent of that employee's annual salary.[28] Another study reported that bad hires can cost a company as much as five times the annual salary of that employee! That's why it is so critical to take the time to hire thoughtfully and carefully to make sure you have the right person!

When the hiring mindset is shifted from "another thing I have to do" to "this is the most important thing I do," a transformation occurs. The entire interview process is prioritized above other tasks and no longer becomes a race to check it off the list of things to accomplish. When we look back on the interviews of the great people we've hired, we noticed that our interview success rate increased dramatically when we blocked a full hour for each session. While it may give you anxiety at first, it allows the time to have a genuine conversation without feeling rushed.

We may be some of the few who feel this way, but Jackie and I actually *like* interviewing! We enjoy meeting new people, having organic conversations, learning about others, and discussing what we do. That's what Candor is all about! However, the world we live in can be very distracting, which makes it hard to sit and just *listen*. I sometimes struggle with this, but I have trained myself to set everything aside, focus, and be present during interviews. If you're thinking about the next meeting and the emails in your inbox, you aren't being fair to the candidate or your company.

Interviewing is the cornerstone of your future because hiring is a skill—and should be one of your most important ones. According to the article "Five Reasons Why Hiring Is the Single Most Important Skill for Founders" by Moritz Plassnig, "Hiring is not magic, and it's not luck—it's a skill. Some people are better at it but you can learn, and even if you do it well right now—you should still work hard every day to improve."[29] In our clubs, we assert that we would rather have an open position than hire the wrong person for the job. So you have to remind yourself that the *only* person is the *right* person.

I remember the time we did the exact opposite. We were looking for an assistant manager, and a young man named Sam came to us highly recommended. When we received his résumé, we were impressed. He had worked as an assistant manager for a number of years at two different well-known private country clubs. He arrived at the interview in a perfectly tailored suit, and he had clear answers to all of our questions. Sam performed so well that we quickly hired him.

It only took us a week to realize he was not the person we were looking for. We had *filled the hole, not the role.* We needed a problem solver, an anticipator, a lead-the-charge kind of guy; Sam was none of these things. We rushed through the interview process and had fallen into the trap that many hiring managers do: we put too much weight on Sam's résumé and interview performance. We hired a guy who looked great on paper and had the right experience, but his WHO did not fit.

A cover letter, résumé, and the interview itself still prevail in most places as key components of the hiring decision; however according to a *Fast Company* article, "They don't necessarily serve the end goal: hiring the most qualified candidate."[30] Résumés and cover letters "convey only self-reported data, so candidates can and do bend their experiences to fit the job description" of the position they are applying for. In 2016, leading industrial organization researchers studied one hundred years of data and found that a person's years of relevant education and experience had little or no correlation to later job performance.[31] That is why you have to be careful. Take the time to dig deep and connect. Don't assume that previous experience in a similar role will mean the candidate is the right person for the job. You might even consider reinventing the cover letter and résumé process by asking candidates to submit videos, create portfolios of their previous work, or find some other medium that allows you to really uncover the person's qualifications and potential. Here are a few valuable lessons we learned from our setback with Sam.

- *Don't be fooled.* A perfectly polished performance, an impressive résumé, and a professional demeanor do not mean the candidate can do the job. Had we been less distracted by Sam's résumé and previous experience and more focused on revealing his personality and ability to make decisions, we might have discovered he really wasn't capable of doing the job we needed him to do. Stay focused on what matters—the WHO!
- *Don't be desperate.* There are times you might find yourself just looking for a warm body to rapidly fill a position, but this almost always causes more problems than the coverage is worth. Selecting the right person is worth the wait! Invest the time up front to ensure you find the best possible *person* and it will save you time, money, and effort in the long run.
- *Look for true value.* Discuss and analyze what value (if any) the person will bring to the organization. We soon discovered that Sam couldn't present solutions to challenges or anticipate problems, which were major components of the job at that time. Had we shared the issues and specifically asked him what he would do to solve them during the interview process, we likely would have uncovered that he wasn't going to provide any real value to our team.
- *Follow your gut.* As human beings we are gifted with incredible intuition, and too often we discredit it only to find out later that our gut was right. A study conducted by Florida State University found that the gut and brain are constantly communicating through the vagus nerve. These "gut signals" are a response to worrisome or threatening stimuli or events that act as red flags that can actually stop a person from making mistakes.[32] When we began to notice the many

issues with Sam, Jackie shared that she had a strange feeling in her gut during his interview but brushed it off as *her* nerves because it was the first major hiring decision in her new job. She was hesitant to speak up since the rest of the team seemed convinced he was the perfect candidate. Jackie thought that if he worked at such great places previously, she must be wrong. Lesson learned: if something seems off, it probably is.

UNLOCKING THE INTERVIEW EXPERIENCE

Have you ever interviewed for a job and then never heard from the company again? Have you ever shown up to an interview only to discover the person who was supposed to interview you forgot about your meeting? Have you ever felt like you left an interrogation room instead of an interview room? Unfortunately, most of us can answer yes to at least one of those questions. This disappointing reality is how companies damage their Credibility and negatively impact the caliber of candidates they attract. Too many businesses place all the focus on the *interviewer* during the interview process, not the *interviewee*. When you put people first, you keep the candidates at the forefront of everything you do!

Transforming the interview process into an *interview experience* is the most powerful thing a company can do. Shifting the focus to the people going through the process is about creating positive interactions with your company at every point of contact. Interview experiences require thought, care, and time spent developing a favorable outcome. According to a recent article in the *Wall Street Journal*, "Only two out of five front line managers are trained in how to make the hiring process a positive experience for candidates."[33] Your hiring process—ultimately your *interview experience*—is absolutely reflective of the kind of candidates you will be able to attract, hire, and *retain*. Demonstrating your ability to care about candidates as people first and ensuring their experience is favorable leaves a lasting impression and ties right back to your Credibility. For our process, we have a detailed and organized plan that ensures applicants receive prompt communication at every step of the way. We want them to know their time and interest in our company is recognized and appreciated.

I remember when I arrived at the club in Dallas; the hiring process was standard, careless, and chaotic, to say the least. There was a complete breakdown of systems, and there were no standards by which candidates were graded. Any of the twenty-five supervisors could hire, none of whom had been properly trained, and the communication throughout was nil! The entire process was dysfunctional, and it was seriously damaging our Credibility. We had to reinvent everything to create an experience that candidates would walk away from and say, "Wow! If that's what it's like to interview with this company, I can't even imagine how great it must be to work there!" So we carefully crafted an *interview experience* to draw out the rock stars we needed to join our team.

When you create an interview process that feels like a true experience to candidates, it creates a buzz in the job seeker community. Think about your company and the kind of experience you are providing to those who apply and interview. Are you treating candidates like outsiders who must prove their worth? Or do you create an enjoyable experience that revolves around engagement and mutual respect? Accepting a job is one of the biggest decisions a person will make, so creating a process that is efficient, upbeat, and gratifying ensures that you will be able to attract and hire the best of the best.

Here's how you can ensure a positive interview experience:

Be Inviting

Graciously welcome interviewees into your company like anxiously awaited guests, and teach your employees to do the same. When a familiar voice or face greets candidates, it creates a safe and comfortable atmosphere to put them at ease. At the club in Dallas, the first thing we did was encourage our entire staff to treat any applicant or interviewee exactly the same way that we treated our members. We asked our people to warmly welcome them and personally escort them to the reception desk. This changed everything! Our team no longer saw applicants as annoyances or intruders. Rather, candidates were made to feel as though they were VIP guests. When conducting virtual interviews, you can still be gracious and inviting. Make sure the interviewer is fluent and comfortable with the technology being used. Be fully present, eliminate distractions, and be excited to engage in conversation with the candidate to display your utmost respect for their time and what they have to say. We also encouraged our team to be part of the interview process whenever possible. They would introduce themselves and explain their roles in the organization. Involving your team, whether in person or online, generates buy-in and helps new employees feel more included.

Sit on the Same Side of the Table

Sometimes interviews can become opportunities for intimidation or power trips. But intimidation, whether intentional or not, serves no purpose during an interview. It is essential the interviewer's posture, tone, and presence do not come across as condescending or threatening. Brené Brown, author of *Daring Greatly*, says people tend to "armor up" for a difficult conversation like an interview. When people are out of their comfort zone, it's a natural response. Brown suggests overcoming this by metaphorically and literally "sitting on the same side of the table." Metaphorically, the interviewer should enter the interview curious, present, open, and ready to be engaged. Literally "sitting on the same side of the table" means avoiding using a table or desk as a barrier to the conversation. We call this "room dynamics," which includes everything from the lighting to where and in what kind of chair the candidate will sit. All of these details impact the interview experience and should be carefully considered beforehand. One of our former interns is now a general manager of a private club and never conducts an interview in his office or in a formal conference room. Instead, he meets with candidates in the club lobby where the warm, welcoming environment is evident. Even if interviews are conducted over Zoom, background noise, décor, camera positioning, and lighting all play a role in the candidate's experience. Paying attention to room dynamics sets the right tone and ensures the interview experience starts off positively.

Let Your Culture Speak for Itself

Your Credibility is justified by the company culture. Whether you are meeting in person or online, conveying culture is essential. If you are operating authentically, your culture should be an attractive company feature. Show it off! When an interviewee first arrives, give them a tour of your facility before sitting down to converse. Share a couple of interesting facts or tidbits that speak to your company story. The tour allows the candidate a behind-the-curtain glimpse of how your organization operates—it provides a real-life viewpoint of where they would be working and with whom they would be interacting. The tour relieves candidates' tension and equips them with additional knowledge for the interview. It is also a confident way to show your transparency as an organization. You are basically saying, "Here's who we are." During the tour and the interview, describe your team, culture, and the benefits of working at your company. In some ways, you are selling the job and your company, but you are also describing the position and the environment to identify whether the candidate will be the right fit for you. It will also enlighten the candidate as to whether *you* are the right fit for *them*.

Listen and Discover

When you listen with the intent to discover, it is amazing what you can hear. I remember interviewing a college student from Colorado who was looking for a summer job. She had no experience and due to summer classes had restricted availability, which we saw as two strikes against her. To get to her WHO, I asked the young woman what her plans were after college, and she shared her desire to be a doctor. "Why a doctor?" I asked her. She lit up and said, "Because I don't just want to help people; I want to help them in a positive and uplifting way. I want to be a doctor who treats the patient, not just the disease." She revealed that she loved the movie *Patch Adams*, and that had ignited her passion to be a physician. I had seen the movie; it had resonated with me as well and we shared a connection. I immediately could see that she was motivated, driven, and smart, and understood the power of taking care of people. In the hospitality business, that's what we do—we take care of people. We could teach her the skills she needed to be a waitress and we could work around her busy schedule, but I knew she was right for our organization because she had this innate drive to help people.

In our experience, we've found that interviewers often read résumés for the first time while the candidate is sitting in front of them answering a question! Instead of truly listening to discover, the interviewer is going through a mental checklist: Professional appearance? Check. Experienced? Check. Or they are distracted because they are thinking about what question they are going to ask next! To maximize the power of Candor, you have to be completely in tune with the interviewee and self-aware at the same time. Brené Brown says that for a connection to happen, a person needs to feel like they are being listened to and acknowledged. It's about being aware of the candidates' well-being and legitimately interested in WHO they are and what they have to say. So listen with an open mind, be present in the conversation, and be eager to learn about the person sitting next to you.

Follow Up/Follow Through

Applying for a job can be tedious, time consuming, and nerve-racking. Candidates are people first, so it's important to be respectful. It is also crucial to keep the connection alive after the interview by keeping them informed of what is happening at every step of the process (in other words, ghosting is not okay). Prompt communication is the linchpin for the entire interview experience.

A few years ago, I applied for a job that at the time I thought would be my dream job. I was so excited that this coveted position finally became available I spent hours meticulously reviewing my résumé, perfecting my cover letter, and submitting it to the recruiter. I was dreaming about what my life would look like when I landed the position. You can imagine that I was quite annoyed when, one month later, I discovered via a posting on social media that the position had been filled. Most of us would agree that, despite being disrespectful and frustrating, that kind of behavior has become commonplace and something we've come to accept. Let's face it: a cold, generic email that says "hey, you didn't get the job" would be better than being ghosted.

Demonstrate the same respect and care for candidates that you would for your employees, because remember your Credibility is at stake! Communication means connection! Jackie always gives candidates a timeline for when they will hear back and what the next steps will be. If she hasn't made a decision by the deadline, she calls the candidates to honestly tell them she needs more time. She is courteous, appreciative, and understanding—and it matters.

Joseph Michelli, a bestselling author and speaker, believes employees should receive the exact same experience as VIP customers so they understand the experience your company is trying to create for customers on a daily basis. "If your hiring and interview experience isn't powerful, positive and exciting, how can you expect your employees to deliver these kinds of experiences to your customers?" he asks.[34] An interview should be a real-life example of how your company lives out its mission, values, and purpose. It is evidence that you value your people and proof that you strive to continuously share knowledge in a way that enhances the overall employee experience.

ASSUMPTIONS VS. EXPECTATIONS

An audience member at one of my speaking engagements mentioned she was hiring for a key position at her company. We were commiserating over the time it takes to find the right person when she said, "I have a two-minute rule. It helps me be very efficient with hiring. I decide in the first two minutes of the interview whether they are the right person or not." I didn't have the heart to tell her that she was a classic example of what *not* to do.

As human beings, we make many assumptions, especially during interviews. In an article titled "Most Companies' Hiring Processes Are Not Processes" by Brad Remillard, a study was cited that found interviewers were more likely to interview candidates based on re-creating their own personal interview experiences. They also asked questions they had been asked during past interviews, assuming that this knowledge strengthens their abilities to choose the right candidate. When there is a lack of interview structure, lack of training, and pressure to hire someone quickly, managers look for reasons to either disqualify the person at once *or* find something they like about the candidate.

Confirmation bias is a typical example of making an assumption. It leads us to see what we want to see and then we look for justification of the preconceived notions and ignore cues that don't match our beliefs. Numerous studies report that interviewers naturally favor candidates with person-alities, attitudes, values, and backgrounds similar to their own. Assumptions are traps that can lead to making the wrong decisions.

To combat the likelihood of assumptions, we have developed a set of expectations that are communicated during the interview process to add a level of knowledge sharing and draw out the WHO. Expectations delve be-yond the surface-level details of the job description and go deeper to explain how employees interact, contribute, and collaborate. Expectations provide clarification about the company, the job, how the position is connected to the overall organization, and the details that aren't found on paper or in the job description. Assumptions are superficial and prevent the WHO from being revealed. Expectations eliminate confusion and reduce misun-derstandings, providing a more effective way to uncover the WHO.

Sometimes the assumptions that cause the most problems are those involving the actual job responsibilities. Taking Sam as the example, we thought because he had done the same job at two organizations very similar to ours, he would know what was expected of him. Had we asked Sam to specifically walk us through how he would handle a complaint from an up-set member, we likely would have recognized that he was unable to fix prob-lems effectively. In order to avoid assumptions, discuss the inner workings of the position and explain the unwritten responsibilities and duties. Don't just show a candidate the job description and assume they get it.

Just because a candidate has watched the video on your website and can recite your mission statement does not mean you can assume that your company culture is understood. Unless they've worked there, they don't! Spell out what it is like to work at your organization. How do employees think, act, and work beyond just their job titles? Setting this expectation pri-or to offering the job lays the foundation for their future success. It outlines the details and ensures that you are giving each new employee important knowledge that will contribute to their long-term value. According to a CareerBuilder study of nearly 3,700 people, two-thirds of employees have taken a job only to realize later it was a bad fit, and half of them quit the job within six months![35] Eliminating assumptions and carefully explaining expectations provide candidates with real comprehension of what they can expect as an employee of your company on Day One.

Taking the necessary steps to communicate clearly and demonstrate care for the candidate's success at your company leads to connection. As you work to eliminate assumptions and clarify expectations, keep the following in mind:

This is What We Expect of You...

It's all about transparency in this candid process. Certainly you want to accentuate the positives, but you also have to address the negatives. Too many times, interviewers don't bring up the less glamorous parts of the job over concern that it will send great candidates running in the other direction. There will always be aspects of the job that aren't as attractive as others, whether it is having to work holidays or being assigned to a closet-sized office. Sharing the downside of the job is part of clarifying expectations for the potential employee. Be open and honest. If the candidate is turned off by your transparency and authenticity during an interview, they aren't the right person for the job. More than 67 percent of employers believe retention rates would be higher if candidates had a clearer picture of what to expect about working at the company before taking the job, according to a Glassdoor survey.[36]

During the tremendous undertaking of rebuilding the culture at the club in Dallas, Jackie and I knew that weak candidates would be run over immediately. Things were rocky at best, and we needed to find the right people who could live out our newly defined core values and mission but also be strong enough to handle the challenges they were certainly going to face. I've seen Jackie "lay it on the table," and what's incredible is how people welcome the transparency. She would say, "I want to be honest and let you know that you may have some days here that are challenging, but the good news is that we are aware of the problems and are 100 percent committed to fixing the processes that aren't working." Then she would say, "We are looking for the best of the best to join our team and help us get things on track." Instead of checking out of the conversation, the interviewees became intrigued and excited.

Now imagine if Jackie hadn't shared those details. Do you think new employees would have stuck around after a day where everything seemed to go wrong in their new job? Paint the picture of what it's *really* like to work at your company and be genuine. If you want to truly connect and build a lasting relationship, you have to start with truth and trust.

Ask the Hard Questions

Though we encourage interviewers to get away from the formality of the traditional interview by incorporating Candor, we still believe there needs to be some tenacity in the process. This requires asking "hard questions"— those that may feel awkward, uncomfortable, or come across as very direct. An interview is the time to ask important questions! It is your job to push past your discomfort and look for the answers you need to draw out clarity. Don't be afraid to ask the candidate to explain further or give an example. "When you said your last job was just a job, what did you mean by that?" "Can you give me an example of one of those frustrations with your past manager that you mentioned?"

A friend of ours is the manager of a high-end private club who always concludes her interviews by asking the interviewee for a verbal agreement. She says, "We've just discussed the expectations of working at our club. I've made it clear that we expect a lot of our employees and we hold them accountable for performing at a very high level. If you were offered this job, is this something you could commit to?" When most candidates enthusiastically answer "Yes!" she goes a step further by asking how they will live up to these expectations on a daily basis. If the interviewee can't give an example, they obviously are not going to be a good fit for her club. We refer to this as a hard question because it is bold, direct, and essential for the organization.

Asking hard questions also applies when you are the one being interviewed. When you interview for a job, don't retreat back to "formality" and worry about being perceived as an aggressive candidate. Instead, ask the hard questions to fully understand the position and the company you may be joining.

Define What Is Mission Critical

What is an expectation that is critical at your company? For us, it is a sense of urgency. In the private club business, members pay a lot of money just to belong, so they have very high expectations! To satisfy their wants and needs, we have to be extremely clear about our expectations for any candidate who applies for a job. One way we fulfill our mission of providing consistent, prompt service is to ensure our employees have a sense of urgency. They have to understand the importance of anticipating member needs. We explain this in detail during the interview and ask every candidate about their sense of urgency. The answer is always telling; they either get it or they don't. But if the interviewee can't recognize that delivering hot food is a priority over folding backup napkins, then they will never be successful in any role at our club. Think about your organization and identify a trait that your employees must have. Make sure to clearly state that trait as an expectation during the interview, and ask questions to see if the candidate's response aligns with your needs.

When you clarify expectations, you are strengthening accountability and forming a connection. You are in essence making a pact with them about their responsibilities—what they will take ownership of—when they walk in the door on that first day. When you incorporate Candor with a clear sense of these expectations, it eliminates confusion and preconceived notions while aligning the candidate's perceptions of the job with reality.

THE S.S.A.T.

Once Jackie and I analyzed the entire operation at the club in Dallas, we determined it was big, busy, and broken. We needed someone who thought like us to help tackle this enormous project…and one person came to mind. Hannah had been an intern for us the two previous summers at Wakonda Club, and the three of us worked well together. Because she was fresh out of college and inexperienced, Jackie and I debated whether she had the knowledge and leadership skills necessary to become our assistant manager. When we interviewed Hannah for the job, we were inspired by her authenticity and her genuine passion for people. We asked, "How will you impact this team on a daily basis?" Hannah gave us an answer that confirmed why she was absolutely the right person for the job. "I will do whatever it takes to be successful, and I won't let you down," she said. "You've watched me adapt and learn quickly over the last two summers, and you know that I won't give up. I want to learn, and I know I can do this." She showed us she was up for the challenge and reminded us she had the work ethic needed to be successful.

Experience, talent, and education—or "hard skills"—are sometimes weighed too heavily during the hiring process because they are easier to identify and understand. "Soft skills"—such as the ability to communicate, take initiative, problem solve, and get along with coworkers—are the key to finding the *right* person for the job. Think of hard skills as the WHAT and soft skills as the WHO. In the service business, we joke that we can teach a monkey to wait tables, but we can't teach the monkey to be friendly, caring, and engaging. Waiting tables is the WHAT and the friendly, caring, and engaging demeanor is the WHO. Hannah's WHO made her the best person for the job because she was hardworking, passionate, and loyal. She was not only a successful assistant manager, but she exceeded every expectation we had of her.

Like many business leaders, we recognize soft skills play a significant role in a person's ability to do the job rather than hard skills alone. A *Wall Street Journal* survey found that 92 percent of nearly nine hundred participating executives said soft skills were equally or more important than technical skills, but 89 percent said they have a "very or somewhat difficult time finding people with the necessary attributes."[37] The same survey found the most sought-after soft skills are the ability to communicate, organization, capacity for teamwork, critical thinking, creativity, and adaptability.

Because soft skills are so critical in finding the right person yet so difficult to uncover during the interview process, we created the S.S.A.T.—the Soft Skills Aptitude Test. This test helps identify the essential soft skills we deem necessary for our business and draws them out during conversations with potential employees. The S.S.A.T. provides a tangible approach to reveal the coveted soft skills and ensures a consistent, efficient way to determine whether a candidate is right for the job.

The soft skills we prioritize for our business are work ethic, a positive attitude, empathy, and authenticity. These traits are necessary for success in our world, so they are the crux of our S.S.A.T. Hannah affirmed her work ethic when she vowed to not give up and to push herself to learn what she didn't know. That was critical for the kind of undertaking we were embarking on at that time. Think about your organization. What are the essential soft skills your employees need to possess?

For us, a positive attitude is a must! Therefore we ask, "When was the last time something great happened to you?" If the candidate can recall something they consider great that happened in the recent past, he or she probably has an optimistic outlook. If the interviewee responds with, "Nothing great ever happens to me," they likely have a negative attitude and won't add value to our culture. Positivity breeds positivity and negativity does the same. In our high-energy, constantly changing, and sometimes challenging environment, we need positive thinkers who are upbeat and keep things light. That is vital in providing a fun and relaxing environment for our members.

If empathy is as important in your business as it is in ours, your S.S.A.T. should pose a specific question that draws the trait out. As an example, a few years ago we were looking for a maintenance manager. With an old building on the verge of demolition, we needed someone with extensive experience who could also understand the magnitude of this role. Woody came to us highly recommended from a trusted source, as he was clearly knowledgeable about maintenance. But we wondered if he would recognize how his work was connected to the success of the entire team. "Woody, what would you do to make sure you were a dependable teammate?" we asked. "I know that when things don't work, it makes it much harder to do your job," he said. "So I will do everything I can to make the job of my teammates easier by keeping things working as efficiently as possible." Woody showed that he could put himself in others' shoes. He knew how his job dramatically impacted others' abilities to do their jobs. We hired Woody, who proved to be one of the best people we've ever employed because he cared about the success of his teammates just as much as his own.

A private club strives to create a community that bolsters connection, so our employees must be able to engage club members in conversation and establish professional relationships with them. Authenticity is a soft skill on our S.S.A.T. because it means "erasing the gap between what you firmly believe inside and what you reveal to the outside world," according to Professor Adam Grant of the University of Pennsylvania.[38] To help determine whether a candidate is being true to their WHO, we will ask, "What makes you different from everyone else; what makes you special?"

When we interviewed Alex, the son of a family friend, we thought the eager-to-please teenager was putting on a show. Dressed in a full suit and sitting on the edge of his seat, Alex was extremely polite and also a little awkward. When I pushed to see WHO he really was by asking, "What makes you special and different from everyone else?" his answer caused us to sit in silence for a few minutes. Alex said, "It is my dream to attend West Point and go into the military because I'm very passionate about serving my country. I take my responsibilities seriously, so I meet every single challenge I encounter. I'm different because I will, without a doubt, turn my goals and dreams into reality."

I remember thinking, "Is this kid for real?" But I quickly realized this was absolutely WHO Alex was. Driven, passionate, and committed, I knew Alex was being his authentic self. He was an exceptional employee, and he made our team better. Captain Alex, USMC, is now an operations research analyst and data scientist at Headquarters Marine Corps, Manpower and Reserve Affairs.

Facebook uses this question during its interview process: "On your very best day at work when you go home and you think, 'I have the best job on the planet,' what did you do that day?" It's intended to reveal a candidate's strengths, passions, and task interests. Bob Brennan, executive director of the software firm CA Technologies, asks candidates, "What are the qualities you like least and most in your parents?" He asks this question to learn if a candidate is willing to be vulnerable and open, because those are soft skills that are important in his company. To draw out integrity, one CEO asks candidates, "If we ever got into a bind with a client, would you be willing to tell a little white lie to help us out?" After you have determined the necessary soft skills for your organization, carefully craft questions that draw these traits out during an interview. Create your own S.S.A.T. to consistently and efficiently identify the soft skills that are pertinent to your business.

Implementing the S.S.A.T. is a game changer in terms of hiring the right people who will have lasting value. When you can effectively determine whether candidates' morals are in sync with the values of your organization, it will raise your company's performance to the next level.

By incorporating Candor in your hiring process, you are sharing your authentic story in a way that leads to connection. You can draw out the WHO, reveal the coveted soft skills, and stay focused on filling the roles, not the holes in your organization. Ensuring a positive interview experience raises your Credibility and propels your People First motto, which paves the way for the next step in connecting with your employees: Cultivation. When you bring in the right people, you can then more readily develop them to become integral to your team's culture and mission.

CHAPTER 5:

CULTIVATION

"You can design and create and build the most
wonderful place in the world, but it takes people to
make the dream a reality."
—Walt Disney

When our good friend Kevin MacDonald told us about Jasmine, we were
blown away. Right before his "kick off the season" speech to the staff at Silver Springs Golf Club in Canada, Kevin noticed a teenage girl sitting alone
just outside the room. He introduced himself and learned that her name
was Jasmine. After exchanging some pleasantries, Kevin asked her how long
she had worked at the club. He was somewhat surprised when she said,
"I've never worked here, but I'm going to have my first shift at the club next
month. I'll be working in the bag shop." Kevin knew that working in the
bag shop meant she'd be cleaning clubs, putting them away for members,
and caring for the golf carts. As they chatted, Jasmine shared that she had
just finished her freshman year of college and was the goalie for a hockey
team in a women's league after playing on boys' teams for years. Kevin saw a
spark in her eyes and got the sense that she was a highly competitive person
both on and off the ice.

Kevin is a career coach and inspirational speaker with a way of bringing out the best in people. He asked, "Jasmine, what are you going to do to
make Silver Springs better?" After pausing for a few seconds, she said, "Well,
I've been thinking about this since I was offered the job, and there are several

things I can do. I'm going to show up every day on time, and I'm going to be the best I can be personally. I'm going to look sharp, learn my job, and be ready to play when I show up. I'm going to cover for people because in sports, if someone drops the ball, someone else has to be there to pick it up and cover for them. So I'm going to be an example of what a great team player can look like and show them how it can affect the whole team. And lastly, I'm going to challenge my teammates to raise their game so we can all be better together."

You might find it hard to believe that a nineteen-year-old would be mature enough to have this kind of poise and drive! What an impressive young woman Jasmine was to answer his question with such passion and clarity. Can you imagine what could be possible in your organization if every new employee showed up on their first day with that kind of intention? What could happen in your company if employees were determined to be their best, willing to be great team players, and ready to elevate the performance of the entire team each and every day? We think amazing things would happen!

After you've candidly brought in the right people for your company, how do you keep them and help them reach their full potential? Jasmine was excited and eager to give her best even before her first day. What can *you* do to make sure this fire doesn't get extinguished soon after new employees walk in the door?

In our organizations, we're all about creating employee experiences where energy and engagement occur on Day One, through the first ninety days, and for years beyond that. We believe in cultivating relationships with employees from the very beginning. The first ninety days are critical in keeping employees around for the long term. Hiring great people isn't enough; it doesn't end there. In order to establish an authentic and lasting relationship, you have to deepen the connection sparked during the hiring process and continue to build upon it consistently week after week and month after month. It's why we've developed our own 90-Day Plan to launch every new employee off in the best possible way.

Too many companies bring in new employees who begin a new job with great enthusiasm and can't wait to contribute and make a difference, but within days their ambition is squashed. Organizations that aren't consciously focused on making new employee experiences positive ones are likely unconsciously creating unpleasant or unsatisfying moments for them right out of the gate. That is one of the reasons a lot of turnover occurs in the first few months of employment.

Here are some eye-opening statistics: 28 percent of new hires quit within their first ninety days of employment,[39] one-third of workers admit they are not confident in their ability to perform their jobs, 33 percent of Americans say their employer-provided training doesn't meet their expectations,[40] and nearly 40 percent of employees who did not receive adequate training ended up leaving their position within one year.[41]

Cultivation is naturally the next step to a thriving organization because after you've brought in the right people, they have to be developed, coached, and nurtured in order to be successful. Cultivating WHO the person is begins by creating a sense of belonging, building their confidence, and genuinely caring about their well-being through the process. It's about helping them see what they are capable of achieving and equipping them with the fundamental knowledge and support they need to be able to learn quickly and take on responsibility. That fundamental—and crucial—knowledge in Cultivation is making sure you are communicating the whole picture and a strong sense of how the new employee, right from the beginning, connects to the overall organization's success. When you cultivate a new employee, you inspire and motivate them, sparking their enthusiasm, ambition, and passion, which draws out their best. Instead of fading on the job during those early critical days, they are beginning to flourish.

When you embrace your new employees, continue to strengthen the connection, and establish the building blocks that will allow them to prosper, you are laying the groundwork for loyalty. Spending time with them, paying close attention and demonstrating your loyalty to them, will lead to reciprocity; *they* will in turn be loyal to you. The first step of creating L.O.V.E.—Loyalty, Ownership, Value, and Excellence—in your organization is cementing that initial bond.

THE 90-DAY PLAN

When I started as the general manager at Crow Valley Golf Club, I was given a tour of the clubhouse by the controller. Then he brought me to my office, handed me the password to my computer, and gave me the phone number of the IT company to call to set up my email address and inbox. After a quick, "Okay, good luck. Let me know if you need anything," he walked out. The whole process lasted less than two hours. I sat at my desk and laughed out loud. All I could think was, "So much for onboarding!"

I came in on the CEO level, but this can be a fairly typical introduction for any position, and let me tell you, it is not the way to start a job! First off, it was incredibly frustrating to search for information or ask other employees for every little thing I needed in order to do my job. I had no training manual, no responsibility matrixes, no process flow charts, no strategic plans to follow, and I certainly didn't have an organized filing system of important digital documents on the company network. I was supposed to be running an entity I knew little about! Secondly, even though it was obvious I had just begun working there, I felt like an idiot when anyone asked me a question because I legitimately did not know the answer. I had a generic job description, a set of keys, and an office. Have at it, Three!

Many of us have probably been there. You start a new job and show up for your first day only to feel like an alien from another planet who is just an annoyance because coworkers have to take time away from their daily duties to help train you. You may be lucky enough to have a short class-like orientation, get a tour of your area by your supervisor, and then are told to follow another employee for a day or two to learn the ropes. Before you know it, you're on your own feeling frustrated, overwhelmed, and isolated.

What we do is different. We created a 90-Day Plan to ensure that each new employee is invited in as part of our family. We understand that starting a new job is scary, intimidating, and challenging, so we humanize the process and spend a lot of one-on-one time with people. We go above and beyond to ensure our new hires are made to feel comfortable, welcomed, valued, and recognized as essential ingredients in our overall success.

You can bring in the most talented, qualified people who are perfectly aligned with your organization's MVP (Mission, Vision, and Purpose), but if you quickly abandon them and interrupt that nascent connection, it's a recipe for failure. Successful companies operate with a strategic or long-term plan, but they also need a short-term plan in place to address and achieve more immediate goals. Our 90-Day Plan acts as a short-term road map that leads to long-term value. In order to establish those roots of loyalty and solidify a bond with your new team members early on, remember the following:

Avoid the Rookie Excuse

Jenny was the first intern we hired to help us with our transition at the club in Dallas. She was a true rock star, and at the end of her internship, we hired her as an assistant clubhouse manager. While no one actually said it out loud, some of the people on our team thought Jenny wasn't qualified for the job because she was young, inexperienced, and new to management. When she shared ideas in staff meetings, others rolled their eyes and came up with reasons her suggestions wouldn't work. When she disciplined line-level employees, she often took heat because they thought she was on a power trip. It was a rough couple of months for Jenny, but after working hard and being respectful, she quickly proved herself to everyone on staff.

What Jenny encountered is what we refer to as the Rookie Excuse, and it is a surefire way to run off talented and ambitious new hires. When new people are made to feel like they are inferior, insignificant, or just plain stupid because they are rookies in the company and new to a position, it causes irreparable damage to the organization. Not only does this kind of attitude diminish motivated younger workers, it inhibits their willingness to share ideas, expertise, and knowledge in the short term, which bleeds into the long term. The Rookie Excuse sets the tone that new hires aren't valued and can't have an impact on the organization until they have "earned their keep." Ultimately that approach leads to new employees quitting early on or phoning it in until they can find something better with another company. Do you think Jasmine, the hockey player, would have stuck around in a job where she was made to feel as though she couldn't contribute or have a place on the team in her first few weeks? Can you imagine how that would have crushed her aspirations and eagerness to excel?

Watch how new employees are treated by coworkers, managers, and others in your organization. Awareness and attention are the keys to avoiding the Rookie Excuse. Spark change in your company by asking new employees to contribute and share their expertise, collaborate with them, applaud their ideas, and encourage others to do the same.

Rather than knock down new people, we do the opposite. During the few months of Jenny's difficult transition from intern to manager, Jackie and I spent time with her every day. We encouraged her to keep her chin up, to continue working hard to prove herself. We asked for her thoughts on key decisions we were making, publicly praised her for the great things she was doing, answered her questions, and gave her guidance when she needed it. We celebrated Jenny's accomplishments with others and acted as a support system so she could do the job and be great at it.

When others disregarded Jenny, we stopped them and helped them see she was part of the team and her input had value too. We want new employees to feel comfortable during their transition into their roles, but we also have to make systemic changes to help others think differently and to change the underlying culture of the organization. When new employees are made to feel special and important from the very beginning, it ignites an energy that spreads through the organization like wildfire. Jenny overcame her obstacles and thrived in her new role. She then became an advocate for other new people and helped them the way we had helped her.

Assume Nothing

When we met Gustavo, we all saw him as the little brother type. He was eighteen, very shy, and just as sweet as could be. He spoke quietly during the interview. We hesitated to hire him because his only source of transportation to and from work was the city bus—which he would have to ride for one hour each way. How many kids would be committed enough to a job to do that? But we gave him a chance, and we were so glad that we did.

Our 90-Day Plan is incredibly hands-on so we can continue the connection and make certain new employees are well cared for. We treat them as our utmost priority so they are never ignored or passed off for someone else to handle. We take nothing for granted because we remember our new employees are people first! So when Gustavo arrived on his first day, Jackie met him at the door with a big smile. He was very nervous, but seeing a familiar face instantly calmed his fears. She took him to HR and personally helped him complete his paperwork. This was his first job, so he had never filled out government forms before. She then personally gave him a detailed tour of the club, introduced him to others, and walked him through an in-depth orientation class that explained what it was like to work at our company, with our team, and our expectations. The most important takeaway of our 90-Day Plan is that we don't assume new employees know what they are supposed to do next or that somebody else will answer their questions. We make certain it is a smooth and positive experience because we don't pass the buck off to someone else.

On Gustavo's second day, Jackie greeted him on his arrival and introduced him to Jenny, his supervisor. Jenny became his main point of contact as she interacted with Gustavo every day, giving him guidance and direction for his first several weeks on the job. Jackie checked in on him periodically as well to answer his questions, make certain things were going well, and ensure he was getting the support he needed. Jackie and Jenny didn't assume that Gustavo was fine; they both checked in with him often to demonstrate their care for his well-being.

It wasn't long before Gustavo came out of his shell and began to see himself as an important contributor to our success. By not making assumptions about the way Gustavo was feeling and instead asking him specifically about his questions and progress, he felt secure enough to be open and to feel like an integral part of the team. Help new employees thrive by carefully guiding their learning process and supporting them through regular connections and conversations.

Helping Is a Way of Life

Jackie and I were blessed to have grown up with wonderfully supportive families. We have always been made to feel special and loved, but most importantly, we have always been encouraged to achieve our goals. When it comes to Cultivating new employees, we approach it the exact same way. We create a caring and nurturing environment where people are lifted up and given confidence to become their best selves. It comes from a place of goodness and realness, where helping another person is not a nuisance but a way of life.

There are real, tangible benefits in creating a culture where people willingly help one another. Not only does it lift others up, it improves the team and boosts the person doing the helping too! Research shows that doing good positively impacts the person helping. It improves their well-being, enhances their sense of purpose, increases their happiness, and decreases symptoms of depression. Helping others regulate their emotions helps us regulate our own.[42] In essence, when helping others, you help yourself. We live in a world where we often don't take the time to offer ourselves to others or are annoyed by their need for our attention. But when we help others, it is rewarding all around and it boosts respect, loyalty, and overall positivity in the organization.

How can you humanize your onboarding experience and help your people become nurturers and parent-like caretakers for your new employees? How can you help them see how important assisting one another is to your overall organizational success?

Here is what our 90-Day Plan looks like:

Day One Matters.

How you interact and connect with new employees on the first day is critical to creating a lasting relationship. When we hired Eddie to work on our golf course maintenance team a few years ago, he had come from another private club on the other side of town. On his first day, he was nonchalant, as though starting this new job was no big deal. It wasn't until the three-hour orientation class concluded that he really seemed excited for his new opportunity. Eddie shared, "I worked at my last club for fourteen years and I was just part of the grounds crew there. I never even set foot inside the clubhouse! Today I got to experience this club the way a member does. I met employees from other departments and got to tour the entire clubhouse and all of the facilities! It's amazing that I already feel part of the team and I haven't even started working yet. I didn't know I could be this excited about going to work!"

Creating a positive and powerful experience is essential for building an authentic relationship and setting the foundation for long-term loyalty.

New employees are never more malleable than they are on the first day. They need to be molded into their future selves, so connecting with them, educating them, and inspiring them is never as crucial as it is on Day One.

We start off Day One with an orientation class where new employees are asked to close their eyes and carefully listen to the following:

"We are thrilled that you have joined our team! We are very selective in hiring, and we only hire the best! You have been brought on board to make us better and to ensure that we continue to improve and advance our products and services! We are so glad you are here! Welcome!"

We do this to present our organization in the best possible light and to make sure new employees walk away from their first day excited, galvanized, and feeling special. We share our MVP and set the expectations of employment in an uplifting and clear way. Eddie talked about his first day for years, because we showed him working at our club was different—it was an experience! Sometimes the smallest impressions can have the biggest impact. Identify and share the information that makes employees feel enlightened and empowered. That will relieve their anxiety, boost their confidence, and ensure they get up to speed quickly. We had a small company so Jackie, the Culture Czar, could be very hands-on and greet every new employee. Larger companies clearly can't have only one person to take on this responsibility, but they can establish layers of managers and supervisors who become Jackie. Constantly creating a front line of the right people who are connecting with new employees from the very beginning establishes the roots for loyalty.

Day One matters! People First must permeate the organization. The change starts at the top, but there's always work to be done on the line level, whether with a department head or middle manager, to ensure employees' initial experiences are positive. You only get one shot to wow your new people. Make sure everyone is on board to fuel their passion, share your company story, brag about your organization's achievements, and give them reasons why they should be ecstatic about their new job.

Handle Week One with Care.

Day One should set the tone for the rest of the new employee's training, and it shouldn't fall off on day two or after. When four out of our ten new employees quit within their first three weeks on the job, Jackie was devastated. She did some research and found that 16 percent of new employees quit a job within their first week and almost 30 percent quit within the first six months! This was attributed to a number of reasons ranging from not enough training to not feeling comfortable, welcome, or part of the various cliques inside an organization.[43] Jackie was determined to revamp our onboarding process and that's when our 90-Day Plan really came to fruition. She equated hiring new employees to planting flower seeds: you can't plant a seed, water it, and stick it on the windowsill and expect it to grow without tending to it in the future. In her eyes, a new employee was much the same. You can't hire a person, pay lots of attention to him on the first day, and then dump him in a position and barely talk to him again. But if you nurture the new hire daily—ask what help he needs, walk through difficult processes a second or third time, provide helpful feedback, praise his efforts, and encourage him to keep learning—that person will develop into an employee who blossoms. Consistent attention leads to higher-caliber employees.

We recognize that the first several days in a new position are stressful and difficult—a lot of new information is presented in an unfamiliar environment surrounded by people you don't know. What can you do to make learning as easy and as efficient as possible for your new hires? We found that by pairing each new person with a designated trainer (someone steeped in the training process) and by scheduling deliberate meeting times with supervisors over this ninety-day period, our employees felt as though they had people in their corner and could grasp their duties and responsibilities more quickly. They then felt more comfortable and confident to start building authentic relationships with coworkers.

Offer and Accept Feedback.

Constant connection is the core of our 90-Day Plan. Supervisors set specific times to converse with new employees, they work together to establish daily and weekly goals, and they follow up consistently. When our receptionist resigned abruptly due to health issues, Jackie checked in on Sarah, her replacement, at least twice a day for five weeks so she could coach her through questions and issues as they occurred. Jackie helped her identify what she needed to focus on each day so she could get up to speed quickly. If she wasn't interacting with Sarah regularly, it might have been awkward to say her phone demeanor was coming across as curt rather than courteous. Instead, Sarah recognized the feedback as a natural part of learning the position. When supervisors and new employees converse regularly, it allows for open and honest two-way communication. Regular "check-ins" with new employees only need to take three to ten minutes, but the key is that these check-ins happen consistently and are transparent. Don't just meet with a new employee for the sake of doing it; offer them guidance, help them work through issues, show them that you care, and continue to build your relationship.

It can be uncomfortable to share honest opinions and advice openly in a new relationship, but there is tremendous value in offering and receiving feedback when the intention is to help one another improve. This form of knowledge sharing is based on mutual respect and genuine care for one another, and it ultimately leads to a more effective operation. It is an essential building block in creating loyalty. When criticism is avoided for fear of confrontation or to not appear as "mean," new employees are not being adequately prepared for their role because they are being led to believe that what they are doing is okay, even if it isn't. New employees need to be molded from Day One so they understand what is acceptable, what the expectations are, and how to behave in your culture. In *The One Minute Manager*, Ken Blanchard and Spencer Johnson explain that "one minute redirects" simply address a behavior that isn't appropriate or suitable in your organization. They urge supervisors to avoid reprimanding employees and encourage redirecting negative habits as an essential part of training and development.

Gustavo spoke with one of his supervisors *every day* for his first six weeks on the job. Aside from checking to see how his daily routine was going, he was also given a little bit of "tough love," but in an uplifting way, when he needed to step up his game or if he didn't meet an expectation. Gustavo was somewhat of an introvert, and he might have been intimidated by a push to take on more, but the safe, supportive environment that was created and the relationships that had formed helped him flourish within his first ninety days.

This constant attention and connection can lead to extraordinary outcomes beyond just engaging new employees. New employees often have a fresh perspective. They may observe things differently and see what other employees are missing. Listen to their ideas and seek their opinions. You may be surprised at the insight revealed from their perspective.

We invite every new employee to give us feedback on our training process. Few companies have a perfect onboarding process, and most training programs need constant evolution to stay relevant. Job duties, technology, and company needs change rapidly, so adjusting training programs regularly is a necessity. When you ask for commentary on your training process and your trainers' performance, you encourage criticism, but you also get a constant stream of new ideas. Gathering helpful observations makes new employees feel valued, exemplifies your desire for constant improvement, and also reinforces the kind of transparency you expect from your people.

Make a point to care, connect, and converse with new employees by meeting with them every day for the first fourteen days, at least twice per week for the following three weeks, and then weekly for the duration of their first ninety days. Ask questions and listen to the answers. Request their honesty and accept it. Here are some examples of what to ask a new employee during these one-on-one check-ins:

- What questions do you have about your position, department, or the company?
- How are you doing learning the systems?
- How is your trainer? Are you receiving the knowledge, information, and support you need to be successful?
- What are three things you feel really good about and three areas you really need to improve on?
- What other questions do you have and what can we do to help you?

Define the Growth Map.

Most people have a deep-seated desire to learn. A Gallup study found that 87 percent of millennials rate professional career growth and opportunities as important to them in a job and 69 percent of non-millennials said the same. That is why a key part of our 90-Day Plan is to create a Growth Map for each new employee. Have you ever seen parents make notches on the wall to record a child's growth? Our Growth Map is similar—it provides the blueprint for a person's progress over a period of time.

A Growth Map outlines the steps of development required for success in the position and beyond. It includes additional education, advanced training, and certain markers to be achieved in order for them to move to the next level. The Growth Map takes into account the person's professional and personal goals so the employee experience can be tailored for each new employee. For example, if you brought in a new employee as an executive assistant whose goal was to become a senior executive assistant, her Growth Map would include all the necessary milestones to become qualified for that role. Each year, her Growth Map would be discussed with her supervisor and evolved to identify the next layer of learning and development required to advance to the next step. It starts with those first ninety days, but as you'll see in the next chapter, that growth will be stunted if you don't continue to nurture the employee for the months and years to come. Companies that have implemented Growth Maps recognize that this approach creates a win-win scenario for the employee and the organization.

Estes Construction, a booming midwestern company that you will hear more about later in this book, invests deeply in every new employee. It has a detailed and lengthy onboarding process, and near the end of it, each employee sits down with the supervisor to create a Personal Development Plan. This plan lays out the employee's goals for the first year and the steps needed to achieve them. Beyond the first year of employment, every Estes employee has a detailed plan that charts their goals and action steps for the upcoming year. It's called progress and commitments (progress = goals, commitments = actions) and is tied to each employee's compensation and bonus potential. The process has proven to be wildly successful and has not only allowed several employees to climb from line-level ranks to high-level management positions, it has also contributed to tremendous growth for the company as a whole.

The Growth Map process shows that you truly care about the development of your people, it sets the tone for "lifelong" employee learning, and it starts people on a path where they are immediately engaged. Implementing Growth Maps for every new employee is the ultimate display of genuine investment and interest in helping your people feel fulfilled, as it charts the progress for long-term loyalty.

THE UN-BOOT CAMP PHILOSOPHY

Some people call an employee's first ninety days a probationary period. Others refer to it as a sink-or-swim trial. Both of these boot camp–like mindsets say, "Prove your worth in order to keep your job!" Rather than see the first ninety days as a safety net for bad hiring or a rigorous effort to weed out the weak ones, picture it as a critical time to give new team members the tools, information, and resources they need to do their jobs well and excel within your company culture.

We execute the first ninety days under the Un-Boot Camp Philosophy. Did you attend summer camp as a child? It was a time to explore, make new friends, and learn new things. Although the environment was out of the ordinary for you, it was supportive and collaborative. There were counselors watching over you to ensure that you were safe, having fun, engaging with others, and participating in the activities. That is how we view onboarding for new employees. The Un-Boot Camp Philosophy seeks to replicate the structure of a camp and is open, welcoming, and all about learning in a way that sparks connection and results in a positive experience.

But even the best intentions for onboarding can go awry when you don't follow through. A few years ago, a social media support company called Buffer created the Buffer Boot Camp to ensure new hires were perfectly matched with the company. It had no resemblance to a military boot camp but was intended to be an exciting, fast-paced forty-five-day learning experience to get new team members up to speed quickly. Even though Buffer partnered new employees with "buddies" to help them learn the culture, their department, and their role in the organization, and even though new employees conversed regularly with supervisors, they quickly realized the goals and the results of their boot camp were not aligned.

Here's where things went off the rails. Buffer hired new people as contractors, not salaried employees, for the first forty-five days and found that instead of making them feel psychologically safe and part of the team right away, they were actually making them feel like they were auditioning for a spot in the company. Rather than encouraging people to be their everyday selves, they found the boot camp was creating a sort of "artificial harmony" where people were just trying to fit in, even if it wasn't authentic. Although Buffer intended the boot camp to be a win-win scenario for the "employee" and the company, their approach was misguided. Any attempt to truly develop, nurture, and acclimate new hires during these crucial early days was overpowered by the contractors' focus on just surviving the forty-five-day trial period to land the job. Ultimately, Buffer's new "employees" weren't confident or comfortable enough to really dive in to their positions early on.[44]

While some managers can be hesitant to jump "all in" with a new employee, it is critical for establishing trust and loyalty in the short and long term. It puts your Credibility to the test and is the reason hiring with Candor is so important. The Un-Boot Camp approach puts the people first and keeps the WHO at the forefront during training and knowledge sharing. When you learn WHO new employees are, it gives you a perspective of their strengths, passions, and potential. Although training will still be training for new employees, this plan of attack takes into account what each new person brings to the table and allows you to play off their strengths and buttress their weaknesses.

The Un-Boot Camp Philosophy recognizes that each person learns differently and at different speeds. Although you can't adapt your training for every new employee, you can ensure an effective process for both the employee and the company by using a methodology that we believe provides perspective and is comprehensive and personal. We call it the Teach, Think, and Talk method, and it includes important elements that carry over from Credibility through Cultivation.

Teach = The WHY

When Jackie arrived for training for her first management position right out of college, I told her I would teach her the WHY. She gave me a quizzical look but nodded politely. As she shadowed a fellow manager, I chattered in her ear about why we did the things we did, why her role impacted the entire team, and why her decisions affected the success of the overall club. I painted the bigger picture for Jackie to ensure that before she learned how we did things, she first understood WHY it mattered. I helped her see that her position as the event manager directly impacted our guests' experiences, as well as our front-of-the-house service staff and the back-of-the-house kitchen crew. She was the link that held everything together. Her communication was essential for events running smoothly, but her composure was critical. If she started to stress out, not only would the service staff feel it, so would the kitchen team, and so would our guests. If Jackie didn't communicate promptly, our culinary team couldn't execute their responsibilities effectively.

Jackie quickly recognized that she was not just there to manage a staff or to make sure food and drinks were served on time; she was a linchpin of communication! She was an influencer of others, and her attitude and behavior directly correlated with our success. She was the energy, the leader of the group, so if she was off, the whole team would be off.

I truly believe that Jackie's ability to be a great manager was based on understanding her role in our organization. She learned the WHY, and it impacted everything she did and how she did it from that point forward. Too many times companies are so anxious to fill the hole that they completely overlook WHY the person in that position is so important. In his book, *Start with Why*, Simon Sinek says people won't truly buy into a product, movement, or idea until they understand the why behind it. The WHY here is still the WHY of your company. As we discussed in the Credibility chapter, the WHY gives meaning and purpose to work. Think about your specific role and why you do what you do. Every position in your company is vital or you wouldn't pay a person to do it! Don't expect your new employees to just blindly follow instructions. Teach them the WHY to generate real understanding and ignite purpose within them.

Think = The HOW

In a People First culture, supervisors and trainers put themselves in the new person's shoes, as though *they* were learning the job from scratch themselves. When you really look at a position and think through each task, there are layers of knowledge that need to be revealed. All too often, new employees aren't actually trained how to do a job completely; they are shown bits and pieces and left to fill in the blanks on their own. The details of *how* are often swept over, and important particulars such as the company's core values and how employees should conduct themselves are left out, leading to confusion and frustration. The HOW is much more complex than most people realize! Think back to your first career job. How many of your responsibilities were covered in your training, and how much did you have to figure out on your own?

When our friend Corey started his new job with a national wellness company, he went through a two-day orientation and spent the third day shadowing a fellow coworker. It wasn't until Corey was on his own that he discovered the many holes in his knowledge of how to do the job. For example, he previously had several years of sales experience, but this time he wasn't selling a tangible product, he was selling a wellness program. He knew how the program worked, but he didn't know HOW to sell it to high-level executives. In his previous jobs, he had a designated system to track potential customers and follow-ups, but this company didn't provide any of those organizational sales tools. Corey ended up leaving the position within a year because he was never taught the intricacies of how to do the job and do it well. His new employer mistakenly assumed he would know how to sell the program and how to organize his tasks effectively. This oversight costs many companies valuable time, money, and high-quality employees.

Are you adequately preparing your new employees for HOW to do their jobs? You might be thinking, "Why did I hire a qualified person if I have to show them every little thing?!" Certainly high-caliber employees will have some previous knowledge, but the key of the HOW is to not assume the new person knows! Think through every aspect of the position and thoroughly explain it to determine their level of understanding. That's another reason why constant connection and regular check-ins are so important.

Helping new employees through challenges as they encounter them and ensuring their behavior is in sync with your company core values has to be an ongoing priority.

Talk = The WHO

The WHY and the HOW are the building blocks of People First, but to take it to the next level, you have to connect the WHO. Unfortunately, too many companies sacrifice relationships for results, and rarely is there a genuine curiosity to forge meaningful relationships in the workplace. The key to Pure Human Connection with a new employee is about truly getting to know them as a person. What are their passions, talents, hobbies, interests, and life goals? In a People First organization, employees are seen for WHO they are, not what they are—the catalyst for true loyalty.

When we met Yesse, we almost didn't hire her because she could barely speak English but was highly recommended by one of our best employees, so we gave her a chance. Yesse was shy, self-conscious, and kept to herself when her Spanish-speaking friends weren't around. Jackie talked to Yesse daily during her training, even though it was difficult to converse, and made an effort to get to know her. After a few weeks, Jackie learned that Yesse wanted to work as many hours as possible because she was sending money back home to her father and brother in Mexico. Separated from her family and isolated in a community of English-speaking people, Yesse was aching to belong to something. Seeing things through Yesse's eyes, Jackie worked hard to help her fit in with the world around her. She started teaching Yesse common English words and would quiz her during off-peak times. They talked about her home and learned about each other's families and backgrounds. Yesse asked Jackie questions about the city, the culture, the members, and the club; and Jackie happily answered no matter how busy she was.

Within a few months, Yesse was working circles around others in her department. Soon, she was speaking English fluently and taking on additional responsibilities with such ease that she began training other new employees. She was energetic, outgoing, helpful, and friendly. Yesse blossomed into an extraordinary employee who I can honestly say was one of the hardest working people I have ever known.

Jackie dug deep to discover what motivated Yesse. She genuinely cared about how she was feeling. When you take the time to connect and learn WHO people are, amazing things can happen. Relationships are the key to Cultivation! Unearth the best your employees have to offer when you recognize the importance of onboarding the whole person, not just the employee!

When you follow the Teach, Think, and Talk method, you acknowledge each person's *value* and spark purpose when you share the WHY. You demonstrate trust when you explain the HOW, and you achieve Pure Human Connection when you seek to know their WHO. All of this leads to not only empowering new employees but gaining their respect, loyalty, and the benefit of their long-term value.

FROM WINDOW DRESSING TO FULLY OUTFITTING

If your organization is just going through the motions during the first ninety days and isn't actually equipping new employees with the tools they need, your Credibility is suffering. You are doing a disservice to the talented people you have candidly brought on board. Fully outfitting the person—meaning training the *person* completely, not just window dressing the employee—lays the foundation for a lasting relationship. This is the crux of Cultivation and is crucial for organizations now and will become increasingly important in the future. According to CNBC, the paradigm of the employer/employee relationship could shift as Generation Z enters the workforce. They learn very quickly and want to be socially connected to everyone, including bosses and coworkers. Generation Z wants feedback regularly, and of those surveyed, 40 percent say they want daily interactions with their boss. Ninety percent of Gen Z said regular face-to-face meetings with their manager is important, and 40 percent said it was very important.[45] If they don't get it, they often think they've done something wrong. "If you manage Gen Z, you're not only managing their skill performance, you're also kind of coaching their life as well," said Heather Watson, a behavioral designer at the Center for Generational Kinetics.[46]

The Un-Boot Camp approach is about putting the time and effort into each person up front so they can be more successful in the long term. It includes nurturing and developing the person's hard skills *and* soft skills to ensure growth in their position and within your company.

We hired Brett because his accounting skills were among the best I'd ever seen. After his first few days on the job, I discovered that his people skills were lacking. Brett was direct, a bit awkward, and clearly used to working as an individual, not as part of a team. So I worked with Brett to help him understand his role on our team and taught him how to be approachable and relatable and to communicate in a way others could understand. Brett's success as our controller was directly related to his ability to work with department heads on their monthly budgets, labor analysis, and profit-and-loss statements.

Getting to know WHO your people are, sharpening their necessary soft skills, peeling back all the layers of their learning, and coaching them through the process is the only way to ensure the person is fully prepared for and capable of the job at hand.

THE POWER OF MODELING

Modeling is a powerful way to openly share knowledge between team members. It sets the ownership mindset in motion. It comes from a place of mutual respect, genuine interest, and care for one another. We work to create an environment where modeling happens organically because it is deeply engrained in our culture and part of WHO we are.

Although we try diligently not to "throw new employees to the wolves," in the hospitality business it sometimes happens. It was TJ's first day on the service floor after orientation and we knew it was going to be ugly. Reservations were pouring in, the weather was perfect, and our elaborate outdoor veranda at the club in Dallas was lined with blooming flowers. Friday nights were always busy, but this one was going to be insane. TJ was our newest service assistant and had been given a detailed walk-through of the restaurant when his manager sat him down to deliver the news. "TJ, I know this is your first job and today is only your second day. We are going to be very busy tonight, and I'm sorry but your training might come off the rails a bit," Hannah explained as tenderly as she could. She planned to have TJ clear dirty dishes and refill waters, which she hoped would make the evening as positive and as comfortable for him as possible.

As we anticipated, the restaurant got slammed, and TJ's trainer had to separate from him to cover more ground. Our entire team was working at maximum speed and barely keeping up with the members pouring in the door to dine with us! In the midst of greeting members, delivering food, and doing everything we could to keep the operation afloat, I saw something and immediately ran to get Jackie, Jenny, and Hannah. Through the chaos going on around us, all four of us stopped and stared at what was happening. With tears in our eyes, we watched Gustavo gently showing TJ how to carefully reset a table. He was walking through each piece step by step as though they were the only people in the room. Every staff person was busy, overwhelmed even, Gustavo included. But he knew the importance of training and the value of helping a new person when they needed it. Gustavo recognized what it was like to be new, and he modeled the kind of caring assistance for TJ that he had experienced.

For us, time stood still. This moment is forever etched in our minds, because it was the epitome of Cultivation. When you show people how important shaping new employees is, your organization transforms into a place where the success of the new people becomes equally as important as your own. Modeling occurs when employees believe that helping new people learn is their responsibility. If you truly Cultivate your employees, they will in turn do the same. What could you do in your organization to influence coworkers to proudly share their knowledge with others in an apprentice-like fashion?

When we met Alisha, we knew she was special. The sister of a former intern, Alisha had just graduated from high school in Illinois and was in a bad place. Her boyfriend had recently dumped her, some friends were causing stressful drama, and Alisha's family was terribly concerned about her well-being and her future. Recognizing the power of a positive environment, I invited Alisha to come and work at the club I was managing in Nashville.

I found a job that would be suitable for her and spent a great deal of time helping her see WHO she could be and what she was capable of, and I believed in her until she could confidently believe in herself. With Alisha, it wasn't just about training her to be successful in her *position*; it was about preparing her to be successful in *life*. When she joined the team, we invested equally in her professional and personal development. Alisha's life was changed forever as a result.

Alisha is the perfect example of Cultivation because she was developed, coached, and nurtured by everyone on staff as she became an incredible employee but an even better person. Your entire team will reap the rewards when there is clear intention to support and encourage others while they learn and grow. Cultivation is a short-term investment that sets people up for long-term success. When you deepen the connection with new employees through Cultivation, you demonstrate transparency and dedication and lay the groundwork for loyalty. If you initially invest in your employees and continue that investment, you build upon the foundation of trust, fuel the ownership mindset, and unlock their true potential.

CHAPTER 6:

COMMITMENT

> "It is not how much we do but how much love we
> put in the doing. It is not how much we give but
> how much love we put in the giving."
> —Mother Teresa

Several years ago, I had the opportunity to tour the Southwest Airlines employee headquarters at Love Field in Dallas. It was one of the most profound moments of my professional life, because it was the first time that I experienced a huge, successful company living out what I believe at my core—*People First*! During the tour, I saw walls plastered with employee family photos, pictures of employee pets, touching memorabilia documenting company history, and colorful artwork with inspiring slogans. The tour concluded in the gift shop, where I was mesmerized by T-shirts hanging throughout the store with the words "OWN IT" across the chest. Out of curiosity, I asked the woman at the checkout counter why she was selling T-shirts emblazoned with those words. She proudly explained that it was a Southwest employee slogan tied to the airline's fundamental belief in giving employees the freedom to own the problems they encounter in their positions. They empower their employees to act on those problems, follow up on them, and see the issue through to the end to ensure it is resolved. The bright, bold letters saying "OWN IT" was Southwest's way of developing an entrepreneurial mindset in their employees. I was so moved by the message that I bought an OWN IT shirt for myself and still have it to this day!

I love the Southwest OWN IT example; it is a simple yet powerful concept. When employees truly own their role, they are engaged, invested, and passionate about what they do; and it elevates the whole team. And when the entrepreneurial mentality has been Cultivated, people actively anticipate customer needs, seek solutions to problems, and recognize that their individual contributions directly impact the results of the entire organization.

Commitment is the next step in Pure Human Connection. It's all about ownership because it builds upon the roots of loyalty that have been established in the first ninety days and paves the way for L.O.V.E. to follow. If an employee doesn't have the knowledge and understanding of their role in the organization, he or she can't truly fill it. But when you create an environment where each person is given the fundamental tools from the beginning, they can take ownership of their jobs and solidify their connection.

Credibility is the outward appearance of your company as an employer, Candor is about hiring the right people, and Cultivation is a finite period of time to get new employees trained and fully equipped for their role. Commitment is a bit more intangible—it is less structured because it's a long-term process and more of a feeling or emotion that is evident in the day-to-day operation. The loyalty between an employee and supervisor that has taken root in Cultivation begins to grow in the next phase of this journey.

When Alisha, the high school graduate from the end of the previous chapter, saw that we had her best interests in mind during her first ninety days, she reciprocated with dedication. As our pledge to her professional and personal success continued past day ninety, Alisha's ownership mentality developed generously. She recalls, "I saw that others believed in me and I finally had the confidence to really discover who I was and what I was capable of. I felt like an important part of the team and that others were counting on me." Alisha may have been one of the youngest people on our staff, but she took initiative, willingly accepted responsibility, shared her insight, and constantly generated ideas to improve our operation.

So if a teen just out of high school can establish the entrepreneurial mindset within a few short months, what can you do to ensure your people are ready to fully contribute to your company at the conclusion of their 90-Day Plan? That's what Commitment is all about, and it starts with a candid conversation like the one you had during the interview.

"Megan, how are you feeling?" Jackie asked as she sat down with Megan shortly after her first ninety days. Megan, our new banquet and events manager, was as green as they come and about to ride the gauntlet of holiday planning season—the busiest, craziest months of the year. It was a challenging time even for the most experienced event planners. When Megan gave a superficial answer of "pretty good," Jackie could have said, "Great!" and walked away, but she pushed deeper. "No, really, how are you doing with everything?" Megan took a deep breath and nervously admitted she had several questions and concerns but was afraid to speak up because she didn't want to look incompetent. For the next two hours, Jackie sat with Megan and honestly discussed the expectations for her position in the months ahead, addressed her concerns, and built up her confidence. "Megan, you will always have questions in this role, because it's not an exact science," Jackie said. "But you have to remember that you have resources and a whole team of people who want to make sure you are successful. You just have to ask for help when you need it."

As the newness wears off for a new hire or a new role, it presents the perfect time to reinforce the connection, realign expectations, and reassess everything that's happened in the last three months. Having an open and transparent conversation, asking the person face-to-face "What do you need help with?" or "How are you feeling about your new role?" is a great way to gauge whether he or she is ready to begin fully owning the job. The person may be prepared but still have questions that need to be answered, like Megan. He or she may need additional training. Or you might have to decide whether that person is really the right one for the position. By signifying this important transition from "training" to "contributing" with a powerful conversation, you reaffirm your Commitment and strengthen the path to lasting value all around. When employees feel invested in, they are recognized as people first! As a result, knowledge sharing, learning, and development happen organically. After the ninety-day introductory period, the time, focus, attention, regular check-ins, and ongoing support don't stop; it continues, but in a different way. It becomes less about the individuals and all about the team.

UNLEASH THE POTENTIAL

In the hospitality business, it is our job to create an environment where our customers can relax, socialize, and have a good time. It wasn't long into my hospitality career that I discovered it was a lot easier to produce an uplifting environment for customers when the *employees* were feeling happy! I couldn't control the employees' circumstances in the outside world, but I could provide a positive workplace for them to come to every day. This is why I make it my primary responsibility to make sure everyone on my team is genuinely having fun on the job.

Having "fun" at work doesn't mean laughing, messing around, eating pizza, and having a dance party. Sure, all of these things happen from time to time, but to us, having fun is about something much deeper. Our definition of "fun" at work is being in a lighthearted environment and enjoying meaningful work while having meaningful relationships. It is about doing something that matters while working together with people you care about. If you can make work *not feel* like work, that's when people are having fun and unleashing their full potential.

My dad was a brilliant doctor. When patients came to his office, he immediately began analyzing symptoms to identify the problem. He listened, paid attention, and interacted with his patients as people. I grew up watching my father elevate his patients' moods, even when they didn't feel well. In my teens, I realized that a medical career was not in my future, but I did adopt my dad's practice of lifting people's spirits. As the CEO, I'm always looking for ways to take care of my team. Whether it's a simple, genuine greeting to a line-level employee or having a meaningful conversation with someone in the midst of a problem, paying a little bit of attention goes a long way. People are always impressed, and often surprised, when I notice a change in an employee's attitude. I know the importance of keeping the workplace positive and how one off-putting outlook can completely derail a team.

When I walked into work one Wednesday, I could immediately tell that Gary was out of sorts. A few of the managers shot me a look that said, "Look out! He's in a mood!" We've all been there. You greet a coworker at the office or virtually and you can just feel their bad mood. Most people clench their teeth and make a mental note to avoid that person for the rest of the day. Many bosses shrug it off and get on with their busy schedule, but I don't. I attack the negativity head-on because our upbeat culture is far too important to let one sour attitude destroy it. "Gary, you don't seem like yourself today. What's going on?" I asked. Gary sheepishly apologized for being grumpy and admitted that he worked a lot over the busy weekend. He confessed that his wife was giving him grief about not being home much the last few days. I asked Gary if he could scoot out early to be home in time for dinner that night. He shook his head and said he had an evening delivery coming in and needed to be there until at least 7:00 p.m. When I suggested that he check with the chef to see if one of the kitchen guys could cover for him, Gary suddenly perked up. "Thanks, Three, that might just work!"

When teammates are Committed, it goes beyond the usual "having each other's backs." Teammates certainly back each other, but the key is that every person comes to work ready to give their best to each other and ready to put forth their greatest effort. And they are held to that standard consistently by everyone in the company. If a teammate is irritable and suppressing the group's ability to work together, then the issue is addressed in a supportive way. A coworker might say, "Gary, what can we do to help you feel better, because we need you to be on top of your game." Or "Gary, I know you've been working hard on this project to make the deadline and that you stayed late last night, but in your current state we aren't going to get where we need to be." Gary might feel better just by someone noticing his struggle, or he might be disarmed enough to open up and share what's going on. Either way, a pact is made to create the best possible team and the best possible culture. If someone breaks the pact, he or she is called out because achieving at a high level is the priority, and that's a lot easier when everyone is in the right state of mind.

THE RECIPE OF FORMULAS

At the time, our internship program at the club in Dallas was legendary in our industry. We created a management-in-training program where each summer ten interns rotated through every department at the club, from housekeeping to the golf shop. Most interns had a particular interest in management, so we gave them opportunities to experience the full responsibility of managing people, processes, and events.

For years, the club held family cookouts every Friday night of the summer on the outdoor patio near the swimming pool. The problem was that members were complaining the cookouts had become boring because it was basically the same thing every week. To reinvigorate the Friday night festivities, we assigned an intern to each cookout and let them come up with everything from the theme to the menu, the decorations to the entertainment. It was a realistic introduction into management, because on the day of the event, the intern was responsible for all the planning, setup, and executing the cookout as the manager. If the chef had a question, he was directed to the intern to answer it. If a member had a complaint, the intern was the one to receive it. It was a fairly intimidating experience, but our event staff and management team "held their hands" and coached the interns every step of the way.

During the last few days of the program, we always asked the interns to reflect on their internship experience. Year after year, the thing we heard the most about was their cookout. "I was terrified through most of the process," one intern said. "But I never felt like I had to do it all alone. I always felt that I could ask questions and get help if I needed it." Another said, "It was the thing that made me realize I could really be a leader." Intern after intern told us that this experience gave them self-belief in their abilities and helped them see WHO they were and a sense of what their future could hold. Nick, one of our former interns and good friend, told us recently—nearly ten years after his internship, "That day, I gained the confidence to do what I do today." Nick has managed and executed hundreds of events for people like Jewel, Hunter Hayes, Lauren Daigle, and the PGA Tour! How could this one puny cookout for a hundred people change the lives of so many interns?

Ownership is powerful! But it can also be scary. When people are comfortable in their positions and confident in their abilities, it fosters contribution at the highest levels. We let the interns own the role of the manager for the cookouts, but we didn't abandon them. Interns could learn, explore their capability, and fail in a loving environment. We believed in them, answered their questions, and built up their confidence. When you establish the kind of environment where people feel safe to learn, make mistakes, and discover their potential, that is when you bring out the best in your people!

Bill Walshe, the CEO of Viceroy Hotel Group, uses this example when explaining the kind of culture his company strives to create: "If my two teenagers are jumping on a trampoline with no net, they will be very cautious. Because if they try something and it doesn't work, they could fall off the trampoline and hurt themselves. But if you put a net around the trampoline, you are creating an environment of confidence through the removal of consequence. Now when they try the triple flip and it does not work, they hit the net and are gently pushed back. Then you will see them try again."[47]

Remember this simple formula:

Confidence + Comfort = Contribution

Building employee confidence is about paying attention and spending time with them one-on-one. Offer encouraging words, acknowledge their efforts, and praise them for what they are doing well. Show your employees you believe in them by recognizing specific qualities, traits, or expertise that separate them from everyone else.

Comfort is the result of an inclusive environment where people are accepted for WHO they are. When people are comfortable in their own skin, they feel respected, safe, listened to, and welcomed.

Employees who are confident and comfortable will contribute as long as the fear of punishment, ridicule, judgment, or loss of respect is not an option. Here's what full contribution looks like:

- Active participation in meetings and group think sessions.
- Continuous learning and discovery.
- Passionate sharing of knowledge, expertise, and ideas with teammates.
- Noticeable improvement in their abilities and job tasks.

Our cookout example can translate into any type of ownership opportunity in your company. Find *your* cookout! Give your people the opportunity to learn and lead in bite-sized pieces. But don't forget to tell them directly when things need to be corrected or issues need to be addressed.

Through it all, they have to learn the good and the bad in order to grow…
sometimes tough love is part of that process.

***

When Josh Ellis took over as the editor of *Success*, he felt that the magazine was lacking experiential stories where the reader could get a sense of lessons learned and then apply those lessons to their own lives. When he began to build his team, he realized that recent college graduates were the only employees he could afford to hire on the magazine's tight budget. Rather than see this as an obstacle, Josh saw it as an opportunity. He believed he could help coach young professionals and set them on the path to achieve their goals in life. So Josh "dared" his coworkers to tackle a personal goal or face an individual fear and then write about the feelings they experienced throughout the process. The personal challenge had to be something significant the person wanted to overcome. One junior editor was upfront about her social anxiety, so Josh asked her to take a standup comedy class and perform at an open mic night. Another colleague was a runner in high school who expressed his desire to lose weight and become an athlete again. Josh challenged him to run a marathon. To show his team that he was in the foxhole with them, Josh did what he asked of his team. He took up boxing and trained nine months for an amateur fight night, because it was important to him to be one with his employees and not *above* them.

Josh's "Dare and Truth" team project required a lot of work outside of the office for each individual and pushed his coworkers out of their comfort zones. He challenged his people in an exciting way that required time, dedication, and determination. Through the process, colleagues shared their personal struggles and bonded over their feelings and experiences. As a result, teammates became closer, better at their jobs, and more fulfilled as human beings. To top it off, the magazine won an award for best editorial series for the articles based on those experiences!

The *Success* magazine story is the perfect example of what can be achieved when employees are challenged in a supportive, nurturing environment. Motivated employees who know that everyone on the team has their back will rise to the occasion when dared to step up. It's why we believe:

Devotion + Daring = Determination

When teammates are loyal to each other, they will work diligently to prevail over any circumstance presented to them. Challenges bring out the best in people! But they have to be the *right* challenges. Giving additional responsibility or assigning a risky project only works if the resources, support, and desire are there.

Look at your own company. Does your team have the determination to do whatever it takes to win? If not, what can you do to strengthen the team mentality or help employees connect more regularly? Consider assigning a "Success Strategist" the next time a lofty goal is set. The designated person will stay the course and keep teammates motivated and encouraged throughout the process. The Success Strategist "owns" the goal and continues to push and guide the team until the goal is achieved.

Challenges don't have to be complicated or as big as what Josh did at *Success* magazine. Whether it is within your four walls or outside of them, inspire your people to live up to their full potential. Employees should be daring and devoted in all aspects of their work, not just when it comes to overcoming obstacles. Determination must be inherent in everything you do.

***

The movie *Hidden Figures* was based on a true story of three African American women who worked at NASA in the 1960s when the US-USSR space race was heating up and plans were being developed for John Glenn's orbital mission. There is a scene in the movie where one of the women, Katherine Johnson, a child prodigy in math played by Taraji P. Henson, was asked to check the complicated calculations of the highest level counterparts on her team to confirm their accuracy. Al Harrison, played by Kevin Costner, is the head of NASA's Space Task Group in charge of the launch. Harrison is so focused on beating the Russians into space that he is oblivious to Katherine's struggles being an African American woman reviewing the work of her white male colleagues. One day he asks Katherine if she can go beyond the numbers and not just check the equations but see what is missing. He asks her to find the answers to the questions they didn't even know existed.

It's a particularly poignant moment in the movie because Katherine is carrying far more stress than the other employees, yet she is being singled out and pushed to do more. She is a widow with three small children, working long hours and being made to feel inferior by her prejudiced coworkers with whom she is supposed to be collaborating. When the disruption among his team becomes so blatant that even Harrison can't ignore it, he addresses the men's behavior toward Katherine. To him, all of these issues were just getting in the way of the team achieving its goal.

Regardless of what was happening, Katherine was devoted, a little daring, and, most importantly, determined. She was excited to be in the flight research division at NASA and thrilled to be involved in such a monumental mission. Harrison's singular focus to get the job done drove him to cut through all the cultural drama and go directly to the person he knew could help them achieve the mission. He didn't see Katherine as a woman or as an African American. He saw her as a smart and talented person who needed encouragement. He pushed Katherine to go further, to do more than just check the math, and she felt empowered. He urged her to go beyond the job description, to think, to innovate, to discover, and to identify a solution that the rest of the team hadn't been able to find. Of course we realize this movie may have been altered from actual history for dramatic effect, but this story does prove why we say:

Energized + Encouragement = Empowerment

When you give people the latitude and freedom to do more, it's motivating! When employees are energized, encouraged, supported, and believed in, it leads to empowerment. They start looking for the answers to questions that haven't been asked yet. Harrison showed Katherine that she was a part of the team, just like he was. He energized her and allowed her to let her genius blossom so she could truly own her contribution to the team.

Being Committed means you are constantly connecting your people with your mission, your goals, and each other. When you simultaneously inspire, cheer on, and build up your employees, you grant them permission to take ownership of their roles. Empowerment is a tremendously uplifting feeling, and the simple acknowledgment that ownership can occur is absolutely liberating, just like it was for Katherine. When employees feel empowered, not micromanaged, they work harder, dig deeper for solutions, and promote the betterment of the company. Empowerment fuels the entrepreneurial mentality, and it is the reason the Ritz-Carlton allows employees to spend up to $2,000 a day per guest to do whatever it takes to ensure customers have remarkable experiences.

Have you ever authorized your people to own their craft? When was the last time you talked about your organization's goals, mission, and common purpose with your team? Give your people energy and fulfillment... then watch as they begin to operate on a completely different level!

***

If you want to see the greatest contribution and get the best results from your team, you've got to nurture the entrepreneurial mindset and bring all three of these equations together. It's the combination of contribution, determination, and empowerment that leads to achievement at the highest level. That's why we believe:

Contribution + Determination + Empowerment = Bold Achievement

A few months into our transition at the club in Dallas, I decided to throw a party like the club had never seen. I wanted to send a message to the team, the members, and the community that our club was no longer about subservience, we were about leadership. So I shared the idea for a block party with our management team. We were going to put on a party for hundreds of members, and the whole thing would be a secret. Members would show up at a certain time, and we would lead them from "block" to "block" on the club grounds and wow them at every turn. Our team began meeting weekly to plan and outline the details of the party.

Less than one month before the event, I received a call that my dad had taken a serious fall down a flight of stairs and was in a coma. I raced back to Iowa to be with my family as we said goodbye, planned the funeral, and buried my father. I flew back to work two days before the block party to do one final walk-through with our management team. The strange thing was that I wasn't worried about the event while I was away. I knew my team had been working diligently to bring our goal to fruition.

Two hours before the event began, we had a moving pre-event meeting. I painted the picture of the experience we were trying to create with every single employee working that evening and verbally placed my trust in each of them to bring our vision to life. I believed we could do it, and I told them so!

Nearly nine hundred guests arrived that evening and were ushered to a white-gloved lawn party on a secluded spot of the golf course. After one hour, the Southern Methodist University Mustang Band drumline led the guests across the bridge to the poolside patio for a Caribbean-themed sushi party. After a while, a cowboy fired shots into the air and rustled the group into the parking lot for a Texas-themed concert featuring country star Jerry Jeff Walker, Jack Daniels cocktails, and hay bale seating. After the concert, guests were invited into our clubhouse ballroom to experience a nightclub-themed dance party complete with bouncers and martini luge ice sculptures.

For days, weeks, and months, the community buzzed about the "best party ever." Members had never been more impressed; employees had never had so much fun at work. We took a huge risk, and it paid off! It took more than 150 staff members to execute the event, and each had detailed responsibilities and assignments. Our weakest employees raised their game, our strongest employees shined even brighter.

This event illustrated contribution, determination, and empowerment perfectly. Once the vision was presented, the team took over and owned every aspect of it. They were 100 percent Committed to getting things done even when I was away. Timing, communication, and teamwork were never more important, and we did it, even in the most challenging of circumstances. That night, our team learned what we were capable of both individually and together. The event represented our transition from a culture of unhappiness and subservience to a culture of empowered leadership. We saw what was possible when we all stepped up and supported each other because we were Committed to one another and our goals.

DO WHAT YOU DO

Working at private clubs has its share of positives: beautiful views, high-quality people, and the sense of community. Private clubs can also be very politically charged, and when you have 750 "bosses" (the members), things can get stressful. Whenever I find myself struggling with how I should handle a particular situation, I remember this phrase: Do What You Do! It is my reminder to lead, trust my instincts, and be the professional I was hired to be. Do What You Do is a phrase I say to myself regularly but also use to inspire my team. It really means: be true to WHO you are and own your role. It's my way of encompassing all the formulas above and expressing my belief in my teammates by encouraging them to do what they believe is right, even if it isn't popular.

Do What You Do is like the safety net around the trampoline, and it sort of operates on Thorndike's Law. Edward Thorndike was a behavioral scientist who is credited with identifying the "law of effect." It is defined as "any behavior that is followed by a pleasant consequence is likely to be repeated. Any behavior followed by an unpleasant consequence is likely to be stopped." So if you want people to lead with confidence, learn from failure, and innovate without fear, you want to make sure those actions are followed by pleasant consequences to ensure they continue.

Here are a few key things to be aware of as you help your team Do What They Do:

Your Birth Certificate Is Irrelevant

My parents always instilled in me that age was just a number. I started my own DJ company at fifteen, because I believed if I worked hard, I could achieve great things even though I was young. My DJ business became very successful and helped me show others that your birth certificate is irrelevant to what you can achieve in life. It doesn't matter if you are eighteen or eighty—you can contribute and have an impact on others. When you are Committed, you want your people to excel and reach their full potential. In order for people to Do What They Do, everyone in the organization must recognize there are things that matter and things that don't. What matters is a person's passion, drive, attitude, capability, and willingness to be part of a team. What doesn't matter is age, race, gender, sexual orientation, ethnicity, title, and salary. Each person should be respected and their contributions weighed equally. Make impartiality, inclusion, and respect part of your culture and style, and encourage everyone to do the same.

Give the Gift of You

Our dear friend Shelley MacDougall is a leadership coach who often reminds her clients not to underestimate the power of giving their undivided attention to others. She says, "Give the gift of YOU to others because your presence is powerful." Too many leaders forget they are someone important, influential, and inspiring to the people they lead. Spend time and be present with your people. Share your expertise, knowledge, and support. The regular check-ins can't stop after training. The relationship-building process and the Pure Human Connection never ends. And a leader who doesn't notice when his employee is struggling or a leader who isn't available for advice is a leader who is hard to be loyal to. Stay connected to your people by regularly asking if they need help, what is or isn't working, and what resources they need. And really listen. Find out whether there are gaps in their information or if they need a Do What You Do pep talk for encouragement. You are an advisor, a cheerleader, and a sounding board; and if you want your people to take ownership of their jobs, give them the resources they need to do their jobs well! Don't underestimate the importance of regularly taking the time to connect, listen to, learn from, and share information with your people.

Complacency Kills

One of our former interns was a marine who served tours in Iraq and Somalia. During a staff meeting one day, we were talking about how to keep each other from becoming complacent in our service efforts. After the meeting, Kyle showed us a picture of a sign that hung off a post at the point of exit on his military base. Everyone that left the base saw it. The sign read, *Complacency Kills*. "In the military, complacency means an entirely different thing than it does in the club dining room," he said. "In that world if you aren't constantly at the top of your game and in tune with everything happening around you, it means someone might be killed." While Kyle's example is on the extreme end of the spectrum, it presents a sobering reminder that complacency ultimately leads to mediocrity and worse. That's why it is critical that you hold everyone to the same standards and do not let them slip! If standards become inconsistent, the result is lower-quality products and services.

In short, inconsistency makes it hard for people to Do What They Do. Here's what I mean: If the daytime bartender doesn't stock glassware, mop the floor, or cut garnishes before leaving, when the next bartender arrives for his shift that evening, he's not set up for success. Instead of walking into his role fully prepared to handle the busy evening, he's scrambling to stock, mop, cut, *and* serve the customers. The bartender can't be great at what he does, and he certainly isn't having fun. When it's time for the bartender to close the bar that night, he will think, "Hmm, Tara's working tomorrow. She left the bar in shambles for me today. I'll do the same to her so she can see what it's like." Now Tara comes in the next day and is not prepared for her shift and winds up flustered and frustrated. That kind of behavior quickly becomes cyclical and is very dangerous to a culture. Whether it's intentional or circumstantial, not upholding standards consistently causes major damage to an organization. You cannot accept mediocrity from your people. You cannot allow complacency to settle in, and you cannot avoid keeping people on task. You owe it to your team to make sure everyone is pulling their weight and equally accountable for the established standards.

If you are Committed, then you constantly strive to make sure everyone is equipped with what they need to have "fun" while Doing What They Do! That is when a person's true potential is unleashed!

THE OATH OF ALLEGIANCE

After my fifth year running Wakonda Club in Des Moines, I felt our team plateau. Though things at the club were going well, our team's passion and enthusiasm had become stale. After returning from an inspiring conference, I wanted to motivate my teammates, but in a new and different way.

You may know the story of King Arthur and the Knights of the Round Table. This legendary leader recognized the responsibility of being king rested with him, but he believed he had to surround himself with the greatest knights if they were going to be the best warriors in battle. All of his knights were experts in their own disciplines and stood for courage, honor, and purpose. As they prepared for upcoming quests, King Arthur joined the group at a round table to exemplify his belief that all voices were equal in merit. Some say the brotherhood carried matching daggers to represent their oath of allegiance and their willingness to sacrifice their lives for one another.

The legend of King Arthur has always been intriguing to me. Back then, it was an autocratic world, yet King Arthur demonstrated he was a collaborative leader. I admired this exceptional leader forging such deep connections among the bravest of warriors. It made me wonder what it would be like to be part of a team so incredibly loyal and Committed to one another that they would willingly advance into battle together. So I decided to replicate this medieval form of collaborative leadership with our team by creating our own version of the Knights of the Round Table. We obviously would not be going into battle, but we would proceed with the same beliefs and core values. After several days of research and preparation, I held a knighting ceremony of my own.

When the seven department heads arrived for our weekly management team meeting, they entered what was known as the wine cellar and were surprised to see the lights dimmed. I urged them to sit quietly as they noticed the goblets of wine on the table and very real-looking daggers placed at each seat. As I explained my recent inspiration and the story of King Arthur's Round Table philosophy, I revealed a replica of Excalibur, King Arthur's legendary sword. I held it up and explained that although King Arthur was ultimately in charge, each knight at the table was an expert in his own craft and had an equal seat at the table. I shared that I wanted this group to be my knights, but it meant that we had to place our loyalty to *each other* above any other job function. It was no longer about our individual achievements but our collective success as a unified team.

I'm sure the ceremony felt a little cheesy at times, but the group reflected my seriousness. I went around the room and invited each individual to take a place at the round table. Each person held a dagger while verbally declaring their promise that these rules would be followed:

- Be honest and truthful.
- Be accountable.

- Believe in yourself and each other.
- When one fails, we all fail.
- Have fun every day.

When we got to John, our golf course superintendent, he was notice-ably moved by what was happening. Before picking up his dagger, he quietly admitted that he always felt like the outcast of the group because he didn't work inside the clubhouse like the rest of us. Our golf professional, Dave, realized that he didn't really know the people around him on a personal level. "I know you but it's really all surface-level stuff. I want to know you better," he shared. We pledged our allegiance to each other and were proud to be part of the same team. When we focused on operating as one, our bonds as teammates were strengthened. For the first time, we saw each other as equals, as true partners. We had been quick to point out shortcomings in other departments and other people. Now we saw deficiency in others as our own responsibility and instead of turning a cheek, we raced in to offer help and support.

Can you imagine sitting at a table with a group of your coworkers while each person vowed their loyalty to you? How would it feel to hear seven other people say they trust you, believe in you, and put *your* success above their own? It is an incredibly powerful experience!

When your leadership team is tight knit, operating in unison, and modeling respect, honesty, and loyalty, it trickles down to every rung of the organizational chart. It paves the path for others to emulate.

When the team becomes the priority over individual success, a trans-formation happens. Employees begin to see how another employee's failure reflects badly on themselves and the whole team. Yes, individuals have as-signed roles, but they accept the responsibility to help fill in the gaps for the betterment of the team. The recognition that each person has a job to do and *more* is what we call "fluidity," which is the glue of Commitment. The *more* is jumping in to offer assistance when a teammate is struggling, it's taking on additional duties to cover for a coworker who is out sick, and it's the willingness to do whatever it takes for the team to win.

Disney Parks, Experiences, and Products has one of our favorite ex-amples of fluidity. Whether you are the CEO or a cashier, your number one priority is to keep the park clean. Every employee knows that walking past a piece of trash in the park is unacceptable. This is the *more* that Disney requires of its people, and we believe it's one of the main reasons Disney is able to provide such an extraordinary experience for its guests. When fluidity is present, the bonds between coworkers are reinforced and the team's ability to function is elevated to another level.

THE COMPASS OF CONNECTION

When one of our industry friends came to the club to do an educational training with our management team, we happened to have a large luncheon for 350 people on the same day. After the morning session, we broke to prepare for the luncheon guests who were about to arrive. Our team rocked out the three-course event in two hours. When we reconvened for our afternoon education session, our trainer began by saying, "I just want you to know that I've never seen anything like what just happened. I watched in amazement as managers in high heels helped valet cars when guests arrived. When lunch was served, I noticed the valets were helping carry trays of food to the servers who delivered it to the guests. And when the luncheon concluded, the same managers, servers, and valets descended on the entrance to retrieve cars, open doors, and thank guests for coming. It was like watching a dance!" Our team humbly sat in silence. Until this outside perspective was presented, none of us saw it as anything but a normal day's work. Our trainer asked us what made our team so effective and efficient. As we thought about it, we realized that we were all deeply connected through purpose and interdependence. While each department (valet, kitchen staff, service staff, and management) had its own responsibilities, we also recognized that each individual area wasn't the be-all and end-all. We could only be great if we were all great *together*. Our members didn't join the golf department or the tennis department—they joined the entire *club*. Our guests didn't compartmentalize their experiences based on the amenity they were using; in other words, the overall club experience was what mattered.

Organizations are able to operate much more efficiently when everyone is working well together, peer to peer and department to department. Companies can raise their game to an even higher level when employees are bonded to one another so deeply that they begin working *with* each other, *for* each other. We call this the Compass of Connection. It is established when allegiance runs on the vertical axes from employee to supervisor and supervisor to employee, but also on the horizontal axes from peer to peer. The degree marks around the edge of the compass represent each team-mate—every worthy contributor to the team—linked together as one and guided by mission and purpose. Ownership and reliance are the heart of the Compass. Each teammate must own his or her role yet trust and rely on each other to carry the team and the mission forward.

This is what the Compass of Connection really looks like:

- Employees have mutual respect for one another and what they do. Each person recognizes that every teammate has an important job that is crucial to the success of the operation.
- "That's not my job" is a forbidden phrase. Employees go beyond the job description to get the work done.
- Everyone knows the expectations; they are constantly guided by supervisors and peers who are modeling the values and beliefs of the organization. Teammates help one another, and ultimately the entire organization stays true to its course.
- Departments are interconnected, not siloed. A unified team works collaboratively as a collective unit.

- Petty turf wars, bickering, and complaining go by the way-side. When you are connected to the group, the goal is achieving together, not winning alone.

When work is about having fun and working side by side with people you care about, day-to-day problems and frustrations are minimized. When employees feel connected to a purpose and part of something bigger than themselves, they can accomplish more than the average person. A team that is excited, engaged, passionate, and truly working together is able to operate more smoothly, recover from failure more quickly, and conquer challenges that would cripple others. Committed organizations are rare in the business world. If you have ever been part of one, you know exactly how extraordinary it is. If you haven't been privy to Commitment, you might be thinking, "What does Commitment really look like?" Well, when we overcame one of the most precarious quests of my career, I knew we had created something special…

Bravo Greater Des Moines was founded to provide funding and leadership to the arts, culture, and heritage of Des Moines, Iowa, and surrounding communities. A few months after forming the new organization, the co-chairs approached me as the general manager of Wakonda Club to see if our team would be interested in working with them on the first annual Bravo Gala later that year. The black-tie, white-glove event would bring together four hundred of Des Moines' most prominent citizens to raise millions of dollars to fund programming and forever change the arts in central Iowa. The gala would take place at the historic Val Air Ballroom with a four-course gourmet meal to be served. The venue, built in 1939, was legendary in the community, and Wakonda Club was known throughout the city for its exceptional food and service, thus the reason we were their primary choice for this inaugural annual gala.

When the management team learned we were being recruited for the event, I was urged to turn it down. The Val Air Ballroom was built as a concert hall and had *no kitchen facilities* beyond a hand-washing sink! It was a twenty-minute drive from our club without traffic, and the event would take place in the middle of winter. The team was furious when a few weeks later I reported I agreed on our behalf to do the event. The gala was a big risk for our organization; it was out of our comfort zone, and the dire cir-cumstances made doing it with outstanding food and service all the more difficult. But I knew our team could achieve anything if we worked togeth-er, owned our roles, and trusted each other.

It took perseverance and a lot of encouragement to get the manage-ment team on board and excited about the event. They were resisting out of fear of failure, and one manager admitted, "I don't know where to begin. I can't do this alone." When I stood before my team, I reminded them of WHO we were and what we could achieve *together*. Finally, panic began to fade and confidence in ourselves and each other returned. We began collab-orating and working together to execute the event, just like the hundreds we had done before.

Over several months, dozens of hours of preparation took place. Every staff member was part of the event, no matter what their position; we even brought back summer staff and begged a few family members to help out! We had charts, checklists, floor plans, and walkie-talkies to communicate. The team was filled with nervous energy but remained surprisingly light-hearted. As we stood together moments before the guests arrived in the elaborately decorated venue, I felt a sense of confidence. We were all ready! I offered my final words of encouragement to more than one hundred team-mates standing in front of me: "When I was approached by Bravo, I knew we could do this thing! This event will forever change our city and leave a lasting legacy for our club. So tonight, as you prepare the vegetables or serve a drink or clear a dish, remember that you are doing so much more than that. You are changing a community, you are representing our team, and you are making history!" As I proudly looked each person in the eye, I closed with "Now let's Do What We Do!"

And we did.

That night, the odds were against us: temperatures fell to ten below zero, the facilities we needed to execute a gourmet meal were nonexistent, the expectations of guests had never been higher, and yet our team came together to make magic happen. The event was flawless. The food was per-fect; the service was remarkable. It was like a perfectly choreographed dance routine, and we were masters of our craft. Golf professionals became valets, the accounting department checked coats at the door, and lifeguards passed hors d'oeuvres as the finest of servers. And we improvised, using turkey fryers, warming ovens, plastic tables, and chafing dishes to construct our "gourmet kitchen."

By the end of the night, our bodies were aching from exhaustion but our insides were bursting with pride and our bond as teammates had never been so strong. We were a unified team with a heightened sense of purpose. We knew that if one of us failed, we all failed. That night, it didn't matter what our titles were, what department we worked in, or what time we got to work that day. All that mattered was teammates coming together to help one another and doing whatever it took to make sure we got the job done. When people are brought together in a loving environment and empowered to own their roles, they can achieve even the most audacious goals…and that is Commitment at its finest!

CHAPTER 7:

CARE

"Unless someone like you cares a whole awful lot,
nothing is going to get better.
It's not."
—Dr. Seuss

When our friend Kevin MacDonald went to give a speech to the staff at a country club in Texas, the general manager, Bob, invited him to play a round of golf the morning before Kevin's speech. As they approached the sixth hole, Bob waved to a groundskeeper named Jose who was watering the course. Bob drove the golf cart over and asked how he was doing. Jose nodded quietly and Bob said, "Did you get your car fixed?" Jose shook his head. "You have to get your car fixed, Jose. You need it to get to work and to take your kids to school. Why didn't you get it fixed yet?" Jose responded that he couldn't afford the repairs.

Kevin watched as Bob took out a business card. On the back he wrote the name of an auto repair shop. He handed the card to Jose and told him to take his car to that station and to give them his card. "Tell Stan, the owner, to charge it to me. I'll take care of it and then we'll get it figured out with a payment plan or something. You need to get your car fixed, Jose."

When we heard this story from Kevin, we were utterly impressed with Bob's leadership approach. Not only did Bob know a grounds crew worker's personal situation, but he also knew he recently had a car problem! How many bosses know that kind of detail about their line-level employees? How many bosses would offer to personally pay for car repairs to help a teammate in need?

Care is the crux of Pure Human Connection, because when you Care, it is part of your DNA. It's the glue that holds your team and your entire organization together. Care is not a tagline or a show to impress others; Caring is the one thing that transforms work into purpose, strangers into teammates, and effort into value. It's the indefinable item that sets your company apart from the twenty other companies down the street.

Jackie and I Care so deeply for our people and the process that it becomes the most important thing we do. Showing how much we Care permeates every step of the journey, and it forms the foundation for which understanding, respect, loyalty, ownership, and unity are built upon. Regardless of your position or title, you really only have one job. Your primary task, the thing that matters more than anything else you could ever do, is to Care. Because Caring is what makes you special. It's what keeps your people coming back every day. It's the reason your employees want to work hard and give their best. Caring is the one thing every single person can do, yet so few actually do it. Caring costs nothing yet produces immeasurable worth.

Care is inherent in the first four steps to Pure Human Connection and requires constant sharing of knowledge, ideas, or stories at every level of the organization. Employees who feel Cared for by the organization reciprocate the Care they receive by teaching, coaching, encouraging, and supporting their teammates. When you genuinely Care about your people, it leads to lasting value. Employees who are loyal, take ownership of their roles, and feel invested in generate value, which is the "V" in L.O.V.E. Value begets value; employees who have been connected and nurtured through every phase of their employee experience can now become the ones who emulate that experience for others. Those who are shown Candor are more likely to be Candid with others. Those who are Cultivated today become the Cultivators of tomorrow. Care is organic, as it happens naturally, yet it is a deliberate practice. Leaders don't necessarily walk around saying "I care about you!" but they show it through their actions. Steve Keating of Lead Today calls it the "Care Factor" and says leaders who genuinely Care are more successful than those who don't. Sure, leaders can still be effective in the short term and can appear to be thriving, but people can be forced into compliance that may result in fleeting success. When it is obvious that leaders Care, employees' mindsets shift from *I have* to do this to *I want* to do this. That's when value is created.

When our Canadian club manager friend, Jon Fisher, told his assistant manager, Clarissa, he was sending her to Vancouver for a weekend training seminar, she was a little surprised yet very excited for a unique educational experience. What Clarissa didn't know was that Jon, her COO, had actually been conspiring with her boyfriend to plan a romantic marriage proposal weekend! When Clarissa returned from Vancouver engaged, she immediately found Jon to share her surprise and gratitude. She was genuinely touched by his willingness to spend his time doing something so personal and so special for her.

How much time do you think Jon spent helping plan Clarissa's engagement weekend? He made a couple of phone calls, sent a few emails, and played along with the charade. At the end of the day, Jon probably spent a maximum of one hour arranging an unforgettable experience for the young couple. But what do you think this gesture meant to Clarissa? Jon demonstrated how much he valued and Cared for Clarissa by contributing to this important moment in her life. It was a small time investment for something that made a tremendous impact on an esteemed employee.

In our transactional world, we sometimes forget the importance of taking the time to do things that actually matter to people. We are too busy just trying to get through the day that we tend to refrain from putting precious time or thought into doing things for others. We are racing to our next meeting, so instead of expressing our heartfelt thanks in a handwritten note, we send a text message of emojis. Instead of walking to a coworker's office to have an actual conversation, we send a quick, cold email to get it off our "to do" list. We are constantly making transactions instead of making connections.

When you Care about your people, you recognize the magnitude of taking Care of the *whole person*, not just being attuned to the employee portion of the person. It's not about helping people be successful at work; it's about ensuring they are successful at life.

THE FOUR PILLARS

Lute Olson is known as one of the great college basketball coaches of all time. An inductee in the Basketball Hall of Fame and the National Collegiate Basketball Hall of Fame, Lute has an impressive record for developing coaches and players who went on to very successful careers. When he became head coach of the men's basketball team at the University of Iowa in 1974, he completely turned the program around, taking an 8-16 team to claiming the Big Ten Conference title in just two short seasons. In 1980, Lute led the Iowa Hawkeyes to the Final Four and returned to the NCAA tournament for three consecutive years.

Some will tell you that Lute brought magic to the Hawkeyes; some will tell you that his success was all about his coaching ability. I will tell you that it is a combination of the two. My parents were close to Lute and his wife, Bobbi, so I had a behind-the-scenes view of him in real life as well as on the court as one of the team's ball boys. I know what Lute's secret to his competitive advantage really was: he Cared. To Lute, being the head basketball coach wasn't just about teaching kids to be good players on the basketball court. It was about teaching them to be good men in life. He took interest in them; got to know them, their families, and their history; and most Sundays, he and Bobbi invited the entire team to their house for brunch. They sat around their kitchen table and ate, talked, laughed, and shared stories. Lute recruited talented kids from all over the country to be part of the basketball program. He brought young stars from such inner-city places as Cabrini-Green in Chicago. Some of these players had never been to Iowa, didn't have family or friends within a hundred miles, and came from the toughest of conditions growing up. Lute knew this and brought the team together in an inclusive way that gave them a family, close friends, and a place to belong. Lute taught life lessons, not just basketball lessons, and every one of his players genuinely mattered to him.

There was something special about the 1980 Final Four team. Every player on that team will tell you that their lives were forever changed by being part of that group. They became "brothers" and considered each other "teammates for life." They loved each other like family and were given the gift of support and friendship that has lasted for forty years.

You might be thinking, "Well, that's great, but what does a basketball team have to do with my company?" Well, everything. You see, in business today, Caring is rare. Some CEOs and high-level executives are more concerned about growing profits than developing their employees. Odds are that only a small percentage of managers have ever invited their teams to do anything outside of the workplace, much less to their homes on a single Sunday for brunch! We realize that a basketball team is different from a work team, but is it really that great a distinction? Can't managers be coaches and employees be players? Couldn't executives place their priority on developing good people rather than just creating effective employees? Lute Olson is the example of what is possible when you establish an environment of connection, support, and love. You don't *just* become a more effective team because the employees are giving their true value to the organization—you actually *enrich the lives* of everyone at the company. It's the deep Pure Human Connection brought about by Caring that is so powerful it can last for decades.

In 2006, Kenny Arnold, one of the players on the 1980 team, saw his health dramatically deteriorate. It was Lute who provided plane tickets to fly Kenny to Arizona to get the medical attention he needed. Ten years later, it was Kenny's Hawkeye teammates who initiated a university-wide fundraiser to raise enough money to cover Kenny's medical equipment needs after a series of ministrokes left him unable to communicate and move his limbs. These "teammates for life" became the family and support system Kenny needed...nearly forty years later. The team still stays in touch and gets together regularly. Forty years later! Do you think what Lute created was special? We do!

Caring is the magical ingredient that produces value and becomes the launching pad for excellence in the company. It must be evident in every aspect of the employee experience. The truth is that Caring can't be bought or faked. It is an intangible mode of being that is either a practice or it's not. Made up of feelings and elusive components, explaining what it means to genuinely Care in a replicable way is a little tricky. But we believe there are four pillars that hold up a company and are the key ingredients to Caring. They are compassion, courage, cognizance, and celebration. These pillars become the foundation that leads to the best possible capital—your people—and pave the way to a thriving organization.

COMPASSION

Jeff Weiner, former CEO of LinkedIn, believes compassion builds better companies. He credits compassionate leadership as the main reason he received an unheard of 100 percent approval rating by his employees in a survey conducted by Glassdoor.

During a graduation speech at the University of Pennsylvania, Weiner shared that his most critical advice to the students was for them to be more compassionate human beings. He explained that many people in Western society use the words "empathy" and "compassion" interchangeably, but there is a significant difference in their meanings. It's a difference he learned from the teachings of the Dalai Lama in the book *The Art of Happiness*. Empathy is feeling what another living thing feels. Compassion is putting yourself in the shoes of another person and seeing the world through their lens for the sake of alleviating their suffering. The Dalai Lama depicts it this way: Picture yourself walking along a mountainous trail. You come across a man being crushed by a boulder on his chest. The empathetic response would be to feel the same sense of crushing suffocation, thus rendering you helpless. The compassionate response would be to recognize that the person is in pain and then doing everything within your power to remove the boulder and alleviate his suffering. "Compassion is empathy plus action," Weiner says.[48]

When you can see the world through another's eyes, you can be more effective in helping that person succeed. By understanding the feelings, fears, goals, and dreams of those with whom you work, you are able to empathize with them and can spring to action to assist them. We believe that if you are compassionate, you treat coworkers as you would like to be treated. You are sincere in your desire to help others learn so you share your knowledge, expertise, and ideas openly with the intent to provide clarity and encouragement.

To implement compassion in your organization you need to:

- *Seek*. Before wanting to be understood, first seek to understand others. Connect with your coworkers regularly and work to deepen your relationships with them. When you prioritize relationships over the need to be right, you seek opportunities to share your hearts, your lives, and yourselves with each other.

- *Serve.* Shift your mindset from believing employees are there to serve their superiors. Believe that superiors are there to be of service to their employees. When you begin to work *for* your people and not think of them as working *for you*, your focus is to eliminate their distress. Walk around with the mentality of "How can I make your job less stressful?" Ask your people, "What can I do to help you enjoy your job more?" "What are the things holding you back in your role?" Then work to eliminate their frustrations and obstacles.

- *Strive.* Continuously strive to be a better person. Recognize that you aren't perfect, that you are a work in progress. Own up to your mistakes and learn from them. Don't be afraid to show vulnerability to your team. When you are learning, growing, adapting, and changing for the purpose of becoming a better human being, you raise your own game and the game of those who surround you.

Being compassionate does come with caveats. Avoiding difficult conversations and allowing those who aren't fulfilling their roles to stay in those roles is not being compassionate. You are actually doing a great disservice to your people by avoiding awkward situations. Therefore, you can't let compassion get in the way of being courageous.

COURAGE

When we implemented our Manager-In-Training Internship Program at the club in Dallas, most of the team quickly jumped on board to help the interns learn as much as possible about the club and its operations. Interns rotated through every department, spending time with each department head, training in at least two positions in that area, and working several shifts to gain a full understanding of every facet of the operation. About a month into the program, I had a check-in meeting with the interns to assess their progress and answer questions. It was then that several interns shared that Diego, our formal dining room manager, was hoarding information and essentially ignoring the interns when they were assigned to his department. That afternoon, I asked Diego to come to my office and questioned why he was avoiding the interns. He squirmed and stalled for several minutes, first denying this was the case but ultimately opening up that he feared for his job. "If I teach these kids everything I know, they can take my place," he said. Then I understood. Diego was threatened by the ambitious interns. "Diego, we have absolutely no intention of replacing you," I replied. "Our intent is to share all of our knowledge so these interns can be valuable assets to our club while they are here and go on to have successful careers in the industry. Can you imagine how much better our club could operate with ten more employees who are trained to think like managers?" Diego still wasn't getting it, so I reminded him of his two-week vacation coming up at the end of summer. "I approved your summer vacation because the interns will be running your department in your absence. So the more you can teach them, the better."

Within weeks, Diego transitioned from hoarder to professor. He was teaching the interns all kinds of things about formal dining service, menu items, member preferences, and time-saving tactics. Two days after Diego returned from his vacation, he came to my office. "Three, I'm sorry I didn't understand," he said. "The interns are the best thing that has ever happened to us. I came back from my vacation and discovered that everything went flawlessly. In fact, the interns implemented a few new practices that my staff loves and so do I." Diego finally got it. He realized that sharing knowledge doesn't take away your value; it *adds* to the team's value. Teaching makes everyone better.

Sometimes the people who train or mentor others end up fearing for their own jobs, because it can feel threatening at times to see other people excelling around you. According to a *Forbes* article, "Job security is a serious concern for many employees in today's workforce."[49] It can be hard to put yourself out there and invest your time and energy into developing others when it could lead to their success overshadowing your own. Courage is the second pillar of Care because you have to have the guts to give more than you receive. You have to be willing to sacrifice for the greater good of the team and share your expertise with others when you might not receive anything in return.

Be a Partner

When we were recruiting Hannah to be our assistant manager at the club in Dallas, we invited her and her mother to come down over spring break of her senior year in college to see the club and tour the city. Jackie and I personally spent two full days with Hannah and her mom, Jane. When Hannah excitedly agreed to accept the position upon graduation, we were caught off guard when Jane asked to speak to us privately. "If my daughter is going to move from small town Iowa to big city Dallas, halfway across the country from her family and friends, then I want to make certain you accept her as your personal responsibility. She's moving here for you two, and I am asking you to keep her safe, happy, and to do everything possible to make sure this is a positive experience for her," Jane said. The vivid picture of Hannah's sweet mom intensely staring me in the face is forever etched in my brain! Jane gave us a tall order, and we realized it was way out of our managerial and legal responsibilities; but after having worked with Hannah for the two summers before in a smaller work environment, we had become close to her. We knew Hannah was taking a big leap of faith and wanted to trust that we would take care of her. We felt genuinely responsible for her well-being, something all bosses should be focused on when hiring a new teammate. But Jane also taught us a lesson: an employee can't give their best at work when they aren't happy outside of work. Thus we spent time helping Hannah get acquainted with the city and constantly asked her what she needed and what we could do to help her. In time, Hannah flourished—our Care for her had clearly paid off. We formed such a deep relationship with Hannah that six years later, she was the maid of honor in our wedding!

The lesson we learned from Jane was that Hannah's happiness was directly related to our team's success. If Hannah wasn't happy with her life because she was lonely and uncomfortable with where she lived, she couldn't be her best at work. If Hannah wasn't bringing her best to the table, then there was no way our team would be as good as it could be. From the day we hired Hannah, Jackie and I never saw ourselves as her bosses. Instead, we saw ourselves as her tour guides, her coaches, and her companions; we were teammates. We were partners on a path to success together. It is the reason we became so close and achieved so much together. Seeing employees as people first means understanding their lives outside of work too.

When it comes to managing people, too many bosses let their egos get in the way. They want to be in control, be the loudest voice and the most important person in the room. Power can be intoxicating and addicting. But trying to have power over everything and everyone is a recipe for disaster. It leads to micromanaging, and instead of Caring about your people, you end up just trying to control them. Have the courage to prioritize your employees' needs over your own. When you focus on meeting the needs of your people, not just your own, you lift up those around you. As a result, they will be inspired and will elevate you in return. Steve Jobs said, "It doesn't make sense to hire smart people and tell them what to do; we hire smart people so they can tell us what to do." This is exactly why we believe managers should think of themselves as employees' partners, not bosses. Kim Scott, author of the wildly successful book *Radical Candor: Be a Kick-Ass Boss Without Losing Your Humanity*, encourages readers to be "thought partners," not absentee managers or micromanagers. She says, "In order to be a true thought partner with each of your employees, you need to be involved, listen without speaking and ask relevant questions."[50] The partner boss concept is also supported by the National Bureau of Economic Research. A recent study found that employees who think of their bosses as their partners are significantly happier than those who think of their managers as just bosses.[51] Be brave enough to relinquish control. Step up and recognize that *it's not about you*! Have the courage to see that if those around you are winning, you will be winning too!

Do the Right Thing

When Carlos came to work subdued for the third day in a row, I knew something was wrong. Carlos was part of our culinary team and was normally bubbling with enthusiasm. It was only a matter of time before the whole kitchen staff was on edge because of his negative vibe. When I pulled Carlos to the side to ask what was bothering him, he shared that he was having a tough time with his teenage daughter. She had a meeting with a company where she wanted to intern and needed help preparing for the interview, but he didn't know how to help her. When I offered to meet with his daughter to give her some advice, Carlos practically hugged me! When you Care about your people, it means you have the courage to help them both professionally and *personally*. I had a very busy week, but the thirty minutes I spent with his daughter were well worth the result of an appreciative, uplifted, and loyal Carlos. It was the right thing to do.

Doing what is best for your people may mean taking time out of your busy schedule to help an employee with a personal problem, or it might be providing a great reference for a valued team member to get a coveted job with another company. It might be hard for you to watch a good employee leave for another opportunity, but if it's helping that person to the next step of their growth map, it means it is the best thing for them. It takes courage to do what's right, and when you do, it reinforces your Credibility to your team and the outside world. Former employees will share that you helped them advance their careers outside the company, and it will come back around tenfold. It might not be easy, but always do the right thing.

It's Not All About Work

Like a lot of companies, each year we host a party where employees and their immediate families enjoy a free meal, some entertainment, and a little camaraderie. To be honest, I've often questioned whether the cost and time spent planning the event was worth it. That is until one year, Junior from the maintenance team shyly asked to speak to me during this event. It was Junior's first year at the club and his first employee party. He shook my hand and thanked me for allowing him the opportunity to bring his family to such an amazing place (a bowling and event center) at no cost to them. Junior then turned and revealed his nine-year-old daughter standing behind him. "Rosalie, this is Mr. Three. This is the man that I get to work for." I have never been so honored to shake a little girl's hand. Junior was bursting with pride, as it clearly meant a lot to him to introduce his family to the people he worked with every day. I realized in that moment that we spend a major part of our lives at work, yet those we love don't get to see or experience what we do or achieve at work. It's like living two completely separate lives. We have a work life and a home life, and we underestimate the power of bringing the two together.

When an employee's house burned down a few years ago, it was her coworkers who were the first to reach out and offer help. The team could have merely offered condolences, yet they came together and organized a donation drive to help Rachel, a single mother, recover from the total loss of her home. A few days later, Rachel came to my office to thank me. "I will work at this club forever if you will have me. And I will work my tail off for you and this team. I can never express what it means to know this place, this family, truly cares about me and my kids."

When Brandon, our valet, was deployed to serve in Iraq, our team sent him regular care packages and letters. Upon his return home, he thanked our entire team and emotionally confessed that our thoughts and support got him through some very rough days.

It is not all about work.

Have the courage to be real people working together *at life*, not just *in business*. The reality is that most people need all the support they can get. We all have difficult times, personal problems, and bad days. When you know and Care for your coworkers beyond just the four walls of the company, you add value to their lives through connection and authentic relationships. And can you ever have too much value or too many genuine relationships in your life? We don't think so.

It takes courage to put others first. It takes valor to give without asking for anything in return. When you focus more on building up each other than building up yourself, trust is established and bonds are formed. But in order to take these relationships to the deepest of levels, you have to be aware of yourself and others.

COGNIZANCE

It's no surprise that many business executives mismanage human beings. You probably have a horror story about a former boss who was clueless when it came to managing people. You may remember that supervisor who seemed to not give a hoot about you. Unfortunately, it's more common than it should be.

We believe many managers actually do Care about their employees, but the mismanagement of their people comes from a lack of focus, or being focused on the wrong things. In an article on Inc.com, Marcel Schwantes, the founder of Leadership from the Core,[52] wrote that most employees quit because of one or more of these management mistakes: not recognizing employee's unique strengths, poor communication with the team, not sharing information, micromanaging, failure to listen, not making themselves available, leading with ego first, or not valuing people. Sound familiar? In our minds, all of these mistakes can be solved with one thing: awareness.

Cognizance is the third pillar of Care, because in a People First culture, awareness is everything! You have to constantly monitor what is happening around you and then adapt accordingly. I remember one glaring example of when I was oblivious. One of our restaurant managers had requested a meeting with Jackie and me to discuss some of his ideas for the upcoming busy season. Joe had worked at the club for nearly thirty years and rarely required one-on-one meetings, as he was a well-oiled machine. I had a number of emails that needed answering, so I decided to let Jackie take the lead while I fired off a few responses. Jackie and Joe chatted while I sat behind my computer screen and occasionally contributed a "Yeah, great idea."

I thought everything was going along fine until the meeting ended. Jackie waited for Joe to leave and closed the door behind him. She stood in silence for a minute, and when I looked up from my computer screen, I could tell she was so upset that she was fighting back tears. "Three, Joe specifically asked to meet with *you* and me about his valid concerns for the upcoming season. You are a big deal to him, and he just wants to feel part of the team. I have no doubt that he left here feeling like he's not worthy of your time or attention." My heart sunk into my stomach. I could tell Jackie was disappointed in me, and I was mortified that I had ignored Joe. I wasn't aware that I had hurt two of my most valuable people, and it could have caused a lot of damage to our relationships had I not gone to work immediately to rectify my mistake.

Being in tune to everything around you has to be a priority, because Caring means you are always focused outward on *others first*. During my meeting with Joe, I slipped up and forgot this important mantra. That is why cognizance is so important.

In your organization, there are three core elements that require unwavering focus and awareness because they have a direct correlation with the success of your company on a daily basis:

Be Aware of Your Culture

A great business leader once said, "Culture has the shelf life of a banana." I laughed out loud when I heard it because it is absolutely true! Feelings, attitudes, and perceptions of your people feed into your culture, which is a direct product of the tone and direction of those at the top. When so many moving parts make up your culture, it's no wonder it can fluctuate so frequently!

Being aware of your culture means making sure your team is always in alignment with your mission and purpose. It means being transparent and communicating goals and priorities with the intent to continually develop and inspire people.

Early in his presidency, John F. Kennedy initiated the mission to put a man on the moon. During a visit to the NASA space center in 1962, he noticed a janitor carrying a broom. Seemingly unimpressed by the fact that the president of the United States was in his presence, an amused JFK walked over and introduced himself to the janitor. He then asked him, "What are you doing?" The janitor replied, "Mr. President, I'm helping put a man on the moon."

If you walked up and asked the custodian at your company what he or she is doing, what would the response be? Would you hear the pride and clarity of purpose that JFK did from the janitor at NASA? We all want to tap into the sense that we are part of something bigger, that we have something better to work for, and that what we are doing matters. Being cognizant of your culture is crucial to keeping your mission on target. Your company environment will be and should be constantly evolving, but at the same time you've got to keep your culture on track. If it gets out of hand, your team's efficiency will plummet and your company's Credibility will suffer. Recognize that culture is not static, and when issues arise, drop everything to resolve the problems ASAP.

When being cognizant of your culture, keep psychological safety and inclusion in mind.

- *Psychological Safety.* A major component of culture is psychological safety. When employees feel threatened by a policy alteration, fear layoffs, or foresee unknown changes, their natural reaction is to pull back. Employees have to feel safe to come forward with questions or problems, share their perspectives, offer solutions, and admit to mistakes without the fear of negative effects on their relationships, acceptance, and respect from coworkers.[53] If employees do not feel comfortable to speak up or offer their expertise, they obviously won't be giving their full value, which goes against everything you are trying to create.

- *Inclusion.* Every person on the team adds value to an organization, but in the real world, it might not always feel that way. Cliques form, confidence wavers, and assumptions are made. Psychological safety stems from inclusion. Any teammate who feels left out is one who isn't contributing or collaborating like they could be. Inclusion and diversity go hand in hand. There is tremendous value in diversity. Studies have found that racial, ethnic, and gender diversity in teams actually enhances the overall organization by incorporating different viewpoints, beliefs, and experiences. While we applauded the large percentage of minority staffers when we first arrived at the club in Dallas, we also felt it was important to diversify. Over time, we began hiring people of different ages, races, identities, ethnicities, and backgrounds. When you have a workforce that reflects society overall, you are increasing the odds that inclusion will prevail, leading to greater collaboration. We agree with Julie Winkle Giulioni, coauthor of *Help Them Grow or Watch Them Go: Career Conversations Organizations Need and Employees Want,* who says that leaders should set examples for how their team should behave, which includes amplifying inclusion. Is this happening in your organization?[54]

To gauge your cultural awareness, ask yourself the following:

- Does everyone in my organization feel psychologically safe?
- Do we make it a point to include employees on all levels in conversations, meetings, and goal-setting sessions?
- Are leaders demonstrating the behavior, attitudes, and values consistently to be role models for the rest of the team?
- Do we offer a diverse and inclusive environment for all?
- When was the last time we talked about our mission, vision, and values outside of a meeting in small groups or one on one?
- Am I in tune with what's happening in my department and my company as a whole?
- Do I regularly talk with employees in other departments and all levels to find out for myself how things are going?
- Do I know of issues happening with my team before they make it to my desk?

Be Aware of Your People

Your employees are the linchpin in your company's success or failure. While working with people can certainly present challenges, it's the connection with the people around you that will either propel you forward or hold you back. As we were about to embark on designing a new clubhouse, we needed to gather feedback from our members about the current facilities and whether they were meeting member needs and expectations. The architect suggested we conduct a number of focus group sessions and town hall meetings where information would be presented and members could share their thoughts, opinions, and ideas. It was essential to capture these conversations and document important comments. Ideally we'd have an outstanding note taker in the room, but when our core group of managers discussed this assignment, we were stumped as to who could fill this very important role. We could hire a temporary assistant or bring an outside person in, but having an understanding of club operations was necessary.

After dismissing several suggestions, I said, "Hey, what about Carla?" It suddenly occurred to me that Carla, one of our servers, was going to school for court reporting. Carla turned out to be the perfect solution! She was professional, knowledgeable about the club, and an excellent note taker.

She had the flexibility to attend all the meetings and was even excited to rack up practice hours she could apply to her licensing. Had we not been aware of Carla's career goals, we never would have used a server for such a critical job. It wasn't about what Carla did at our club; it was about WHO Carla was beyond our four walls. We knew we could trust her with this very important assignment.

There have been many times in my career that, like the Carla example, my knowledge of employee skills, hobbies, and interests outside of work came to the rescue. And every time, the employees I went to for help felt valued because I saw them for much more than just their position at the club. That's reason enough to take the time to develop relationships with coworkers and know them on a deeper level. Remember, it's all about connection! Be aware of your people, how they are feeling, what their dreams are, what challenges they are having, and what gets them out of bed every morning. When you are constantly in tune with your people, you will be operating with trust, respect, and understanding.

As you strive to monitor your awareness of your people and relationships, ask yourself these questions:

- How well do my coworkers know WHO I am?
- How well do I know the people I work with?
- Do I know the first *and* *last* names of everyone in my department
- Do I know if my coworkers have spouses, children, or pets? If yes, what are their names?
- When was the last time I talked with my coworkers about something other than work?

Be Aware of Yourself

When Jackie and I were catching up with a friend recently, we asked her how things were going with her new boss. "Frank is great!" she said. "I guess the best way to describe the change is that when any of us saw Ted, our old CEO, walking toward our office, we all acted busy with very important work and prayed he wouldn't stop at our desk. Now when we see Frank walking toward our office, we smile and hope he stops to chat. It's like Ted was an inhale and Frank is an exhale."

Have you ever realized that you are a manager of energy? Do you know that you have the power to positively or negatively impact those around you on a daily basis? Ted, whether he meant to be or not, was an energy-sucking manager. His people tensed up, panicked, and desperately tried to avoid his complaining, criticizing, and micromanaging. Frank is an energy giver. He is upbeat, asks questions, shares stories, and offers encouragement. Ted took energy from his people and Frank gives energy to his people. Ask yourself, are you an inhale or an exhale?

Self-awareness is being conscious of how you come across to others and is equally as important as what you are saying or doing (if not more so!). When you are cognizant, you Care how you impact your teammates and how your messages are received, and you are constantly self-monitoring your approach and performance. To give your best to your teammates, you have to be aware of yourself. It's ridiculous to think that you don't have flaws or weaknesses. No one is perfect 100 percent of the time. Stress, lack of time, change, and endless responsibilities can take a toll on people. But making a conscious effort to stop and analyze your own actions, emotions, and communication gives you a different perspective and allows you to make adjustments to maximize performance.

Self-awareness takes practice and focus. When it is employed regularly by everyone on the team, it becomes the lifeblood of a thriving organization. The more self-awareness is practiced, the more self-improvement takes place. It's the reason we developed this Self-Awareness Checklist:

- Am I a boss or a partner?
- How do I make my teammates feel when I walk into the room?
- When was the last time I publicly admitted making a mistake?
- Am I delivering on the promises I am making?
- Am I setting an example of how to think, behave, and communicate to my team?
- What could I have done differently today to get a better result?
- Am I listening to my teammates?

- When was the last time someone on my team pushed back on one of my ideas? How did I respond?
- Did I allow my emotions to get the best of me recently?
- What could I do to better support my coworkers?

The key to cognizance is that it's a purposeful practice. It's not something you do every now and again; it is a conscious state of being. Always monitoring what is going on with your culture, your people, and yourself ensures that you are connected at the deepest levels and appreciating your employees in the most powerful way.

CELEBRATION

When President George W. Bush played golf at the club, we made every effort to ensure that he blended in. The Secret Service kept us hopping, but we worked together as seamlessly as possible. I had developed a pretty good relationship with Tom, one of the lead Secret Service guys, so I asked him for a small favor. After he confirmed my request, I went looking for Kyle, the intern and former marine we mentioned earlier, who was now pursuing a career in the hospitality industry. He was having an exceptional summer thus far and had just completed a hectic eighty-hour workweek. Kyle had gone above and beyond to help out on numerous occasions, and I thought he deserved a little celebration for his hard work. When I found Kyle, all I told him was, "I need you to do something for me. I need you to go to the snack house on the golf course. When you get there, find Tom."

When Kyle arrived at the snack house, he found Tom, who immediately whisked him over to a table where the former president was sitting. President Bush stood up, shook Kyle's hand, and asked him a series of questions about his platoon, his missions, and where he was from. After a few minutes of conversation and a photo, President Bush asked Kyle if he would do something for him, to which Kyle enthusiastically accepted with a "Yes, sir, anything, sir."

"Kyle, I want you to do something for me when you get off work today. I want you to call your mother and thank her for me. I want her to know how much I appreciate her sacrifice and what it took for her and your family to have you away so long," he said.

I was in a meeting in my office with a few of the managers when suddenly there was a knock at my door. Kyle opened the door and was so emotional he could barely speak. When Kyle shared his brief encounter with President Bush, it wasn't long before all of us had tears streaming down our faces. He walked over, hugged me, and said, "Three, I will never be able to express to you what that meant to me. Thank you."

Meeting President Bush was one of the most memorable moments in Kyle's life. He had the opportunity to meet his commander in chief. He looked him in the eye, shook his hand, and heard him say, "Thank you for your sacrifice." The fact that President Bush knew exactly where Kyle's platoon had been, even before Kyle told him, and that he personally thanked Kyle (and his mother!) for his service was the greatest sign of appreciation he could have received.

Celebration is the final pillar of Caring, and it is by far the most powerful in engaging, retaining, and motivating employees. When employees are genuinely appreciated and their efforts recognized in a way that speaks to their WHO, it fuels their purpose, validates their contribution, and increases their value.

To be completely honest, I arranged for Kyle to meet President Bush not because of the work that Kyle had done so far on his internship. Yes, he was doing a great job and working hard, but as I got to know him, I learned more about his experience as a marine and dedication to his country. I knew that meeting President Bush would touch him to his core. And it did. After Kyle's meeting with President Bush, he worked even harder, was more passionate, and produced more value than he did before. The story gets even better. Kyle's small hometown in Indiana got wind of his unexpected meeting with the former president, and it became the cover story of the local newspaper! Kyle and his family were celebrated in their community in an incredibly special way.

Have you ever wanted to do something special for one of your employees but talked yourself out of it because you were too busy? So have I. Here's a reminder for all of us: it took about ten minutes of my time to do something for Kyle that he will remember for the rest of his life.

There's a lot of talk in the business world these days about creating an environment of gratitude, employee recognition, and rewarding employees. To us, it always seems to be overcomplicated when really it's quite simple. An environment of gratitude is one where people's contribution and efforts are appreciated. Recognition is thanking someone and acknowledging their work. Rewards are prizes, payments, or something else concrete to encourage repeat behavior. We uncomplicated the process by merging all of these into one pillar: celebration. When you celebrate a teammate, you simply pause from the day-to-day chaos to rejoice, commemorate, and recognize something positive. It makes work lighter and more fulfilling. Celebrating is taking a moment to really see people and acknowledge their contribution.

Celebration is a calculated practice that is invaluable to people and organizations. O.C. Tanner, an employee recognition company, says, "When people are appreciated, they're inspired. Inspired people produce great work that helps companies grow." Kyle's moment of recognition made him more motivated than I had ever seen him. In return, I was inspired as well. I wanted to find ways to celebrate more people more often. And most importantly, I wanted celebration and joy to be at the core of our culture.

On the last night of our biggest golf tournament of the year, our team was exhausted after nonstop activities going from 7:00 a.m. until midnight for three days straight. When the members left, we ordered pizza and sat together eating and debriefing everything that transpired. When I shared that members were raving to me about the event, we all clapped, cheered, and slapped high fives to celebrate all that we had accomplished. As we said our goodbyes to head home, Carter, our newest employee, stopped to tell me how much it meant to him that we took the time to acknowledge all the effort that went in to the golf tournament. "My old boss never did stuff like that. We didn't celebrate anything. Whenever we did something great, he always made a comment about something we could have done better," Carter said. He went on to say that working in a place where nothing was ever good enough was unfulfilling and frustrating. It was the reason he left that job and came to work at our club.

Carter's comments stuck with me. No one wants to feel unappreciated. So ask yourself, do you take the time to celebrate your people and their accomplishments? When an employee excitedly announces they made a $10,000 sale, do you smile, clap, and yell "Way to go!" or do you grumble something like, "Well, we're still $3 million behind our budget so get back to work!"?

This may seem like petty stuff, but research indicates that employees across the board are frustrated by a lack of appreciation from their bosses and supervisors. The *Harvard Business Review* reported the average employee said it had been fifty days since they last felt recognized for anything they did at work. A Gallup study found that employees who don't feel adequately recognized are twice as likely to quit in the next year. Forty percent of American workers say they would put more effort into their jobs if their employer recognized them more often.[55]

So if recognition motivates employees, gives them a sense of accomplishment, helps them feel valued for their work, and costs little or nothing, why don't more bosses make it a priority? We believe it's because managers are too focused on *tasks* and should be more focused on *people.*

Bring celebration into your organization with these three simple steps—gratitude, recognition, and rewards:

Gratitude

"Showing a little gratitude in the office could be the simplest, yet most effective way to boost morale and promote a healthy culture," says Amy Morin, an international bestselling mental strength author.[56] She says all too often, bosses are thinking employees should be grateful to have jobs and employees are thinking bosses should be grateful they are willing to work for such unappreciative jerks!

The fact is a lack of appreciation can lead to a toxic work culture and underperforming employees. When you choose to be grateful (and it is a choice) for the efforts of your employees, you are living true to the People First mentality. Remember, employees have a choice in where they work and how much effort they put forth. Saying "thank you" goes a long way, but the key is that it must be genuine and meaningful to be effective.

In my early years of managing clubs, I once had an employee tell me the staff was feeling underappreciated and wished I thanked them more often. It's the reason that I started the practice of randomly walking through individual departments to look employees in the eyes and shake their hands while I thanked them for their hard work that day. I know how much it means to be personally recognized by a supervisor after a busy day or big event.

When you Care, you make it a point to express your thankfulness for the effort, contribution, and input of your coworkers. Not only does gratitude enhance your culture, research says it also increases employee productivity and job satisfaction, improves well-being, and reduces stress in the workplace.[57] To boost your sense of gratitude, think about what it takes to run your department every day. Then think about what would happen if one or two of your employees weren't there. Who would cover those duties and how would it impact your department? When you look through the lens of gratitude, you choose to see and appreciate each individual's daily contribution to the organization.

Recognition

When things finally began to change at the club in Dallas, we realized we had a lot of people who deserved recognition. So many teammates were taking initiative and working harder than ever before to help us get things on the right track. Our management team came up with the idea of a surprise awards show to recognize as many employees as possible. We called a mandatory all-staff meeting. When everyone showed up, they were shocked to see our management team in sequined black dresses and tuxedos. We acknowledged the achievements of each department before handing out the Department of the Year, Leader of the Year, and Rock Star Awards to deserving recipients. The energy in the room was electric as the heralded employees stood in front of their coworkers beaming with pride. Recognition can be big, like our annual awards show, or recognition can be small. It can be little things like a handwritten note, a thank-you card, or a shout-out during a meeting; or it can be stopping by someone's office to say that you loved their presentation that morning and that they did a great job. Both can be effective, but the key is that recognition has to be authentic, meaningful, and specific...and sometimes spontaneous. A smug "thanks" or a cheesy balloon that says "we appreciate you" tend to do more harm than good. Make sure when you're giving praise, it is genuine. For recognition to be meaningful, take a few seconds to think about what would mean the most to that person.

When you connect with your coworkers and know them on a personal level, you recognize them in more significant ways. With Kyle, I could have simply pulled him aside to tell him he was doing a great job, but arranging for him to meet President Bush was far more meaningful to him. Be specific by saying exactly what you are acknowledging the person for, don't just mutter general statements. Instead of "Great job yesterday," say, "Laura, thank you for staying late last night to make sure those packages went out before the deadline."

Rewards

In our opinion, rewards can be the trickiest part of celebration, because to be effective, they have to be relevant and appropriate to the person you are rewarding. For example, every Thanksgiving we gave each employee a ten-pound turkey as a reward for working the holiday. We thought we were really doing something great for our employees, until one year, the chef saw several turkeys in the dumpster! We didn't take into account that as we diversified our team, we had more college kids and employees of different cultures, so the reward wasn't as relevant to them as it was in the past. Everyone is different, so some employees might be thrilled with monetary rewards while others could care less about the money. One employee might be delighted to be rewarded with a software class to sharpen his skills while another employee might take offense to the idea that you think he needs improvement.

Rewards also have to be appropriate. If an employee achieves something small but receives a big reward, it can create animosity among the staff. Or if an employee achieves something big but gets an undersized reward, it can defeat the person entirely. Thus rewards can be tricky. The key is relevancy, and if you don't know what kind of reward an employee would welcome or deem worthy, ask him or her! When our friend Jon Fisher wanted to reward one of his employees, he asked her a few questions candidly. Miranda was the main attendant at the club's snack house on the golf course, and when her counterpart had to be let go suddenly, Miranda had to cover long hours, seven days a week, for nearly three weeks. When she could finally have a day off, Jon asked her what she was going to do that day. "Clean my house!" she said. On the morning of her day off, Jon called Miranda to let her know he had hired a cleaning crew that would be arriving at her house in fifteen minutes and she was booked for a day full of treatments at the spa across town! In this case, the reward served its purpose and then some! When done right, rewards go a long way in showing employees you Care.

Celebrating employees is a low-cost initiative for creating a positive, uplifting work environment. That allows an optimal employee experience, increased productivity, and a higher retention rate. When you appreciate employees in ways that are meaningful and appropriate, you keep the connection alive. You inspire and encourage your people to do the right things, and you reinforce the desired behavior to others in the organization.

Remember, don't overcomplicate celebration! It could be a ten-second round of applause, a five-second handshake, or a two-second "cheers" with your coffee mugs. It doesn't have to be elaborate; it just has to be authentic. Make it a priority to stop, think, and acknowledge your people, because doing something is better than doing nothing. When you Care, you know the power of celebration. You are a grateful leader who seeks opportunities to make employees feel valued.

***

In short, compassion, courage, cognizance, and celebration are all about the people! For too long, business leaders have been programmed to believe that caring for employees is a sign of weakness, that their focus should be on their personal accomplishment. But when you Care, the priority is shifted to *the other person.* That's when real value is unlocked and your organization's most precious intellectual assets transform it from a company that is surviving to one that is thriving!

CHAPTER 8:

THRIVING

"None of us is as smart as **all** of us."
—Ken Blanchard

Estes Construction, the company we mentioned in the Cultivation chapter, is operating at the top of its game. If you recall, the company requires every employee to create an annual Growth Map—believing that dynamic people and an inspiring culture lead to a great client experience with successful outcomes. Four core values called "the Estes Way" are part of the daily conversation; they're woven into everything it does and are used as a baseline for every decision made. Estes Construction is known as an employer of choice in their community and as a result receives hundreds of applications for open positions within a matter of days. Estes further reinforces its Credibility as it strives to make every candidate experience positive and enjoyable by ensuring prospective employees are appreciated, informed, and carefully guided through the interview and hiring process. Estes hires slowly and deliberately. Hiring is taken so seriously that executives conduct the final interview for key positions over dinner with the candidate and his or her partner/spouse if he or she has one. Questions are answered with honesty and transparency while expectations of the position and the future working relationship are detailed to ensure a great employee experience from Day One.

Estes Construction heavily invests in training its people. College students participating in its "Pathway to President" program receive upward of $300,000 in training, education, and development during this three-year program. Growth is a constant focus; employee bonuses and commissions are strictly based on whether the goals in their Personal Improvement Plans are achieved. For the past twelve years, Estes employees have earned the maximum amount possible for bonus and profit-sharing opportunities! Its people are paid in the top quartile of the construction industry, and the company performs in the top quartile of the industry year after year. When employees are winning, the company is winning—the actual meaning of People First!

When you follow the five steps to Pure Human Connection as Estes Construction does, it motivates and elevates your people—the best possible capital you have! Employees who are treated as valuable assets operate as invested "owners" of the business. Because these precious assets impact every facet of your organization, they produce the best possible results. Estes Construction proves that prioritizing connection is the path to success!

THE BEST POSSIBLE CAPITAL

Strive to create loyalty, ownership, and value so your employees are able to operate at their highest potential. This leads to excellence—the "E" in L.O.V.E.! Unquestionably, the Estes team is operating with excellence! By implementing all five steps—Credibility, Candor, Cultivation, Commitment, and Care—you form a circle of L.O.V.E. through Pure Human Connection. When you love your people, they will love you in return! A culture of L.O.V.E. yields a thriving organization. Successful companies are made up of successful human beings. That's why employees who feel genuinely cared for by the company are:

- recognized and rewarded as key contributors by the organization
- engaged in work that speaks to their purpose
- deeply connected with their fellow coworkers
- And they create organizations that:
- evolve, change, and generate momentum more rapidly
- overcome obstacles and challenges more swiftly
- operate at the highest levels of efficiency

- respond to competitors' tactics proactively rather than reactively
- become so closely bonded that communication, collaboration, and knowledge sharing is uncanny and the norm

Estes Construction oozes Credibility because it lives and breathes its Mission, Vision, and Purpose. Estes hires with Candor and Cultivates new employees like loving parents who want the best for their children. Estes believes in its MVP so deeply that one-third of the company's gross profits goes to compensation. Some might call that crazy spending, but Estes calls it smart investment! In the last eight years, Estes Construction has grown fourfold. The CEO credits that success to how employee development is prioritized. "We contend with multimillion-dollar companies because construction is a highly competitive industry. We believe the only way we can impact our result is by having the best possible people who are constantly outlearning our competitors," said Kent Pilcher, the CEO of Estes Construction.

So think about this: When we take as much interest in someone as they take in us, we naturally reciprocate, right? Isn't that something we should be doing for our people? Doesn't it seem logical that employees will generate results equal to or greater than the amount of investment the company is making in them? The more you focus on your employees, the more long-term value they will produce!

Today's workers are seeking opportunities to gain experience, build their knowledge bases, and develop skills that will help them advance more quickly in their careers. It's not just about title and salary these days. A recent Gallup study found that 87 percent of millennials prioritized professional growth and development opportunities in a job, while 69 percent of non-millennials said the same.[58] If we learn one thing from Estes Construction, it's that making the investment in your people pays off! Are you truly investing in *your* human capital?

In our fast-paced, competitive world, the only way to stay ahead of the competition is to outsmart them. The only way to outsmart the competition is to *outlearn* the competition. If you don't have the most educated, efficient, and genuinely inspired team possible, you will always be one step behind.

FUELED BY FEEDBACK

In an environment of connection, learning happens through transparent conversations with colleagues on all levels. Feedback is critical to the learning process, but it can't be a one-way street.

Our friend Anna-Vija started her own marketing company a few years ago. As her business began to take off and people were added to her team, it was difficult communicating her high-level expectations to her employees without coming across as harsh and demanding. Anna-Vija soon found herself spending too much time smoothing over misunderstandings and accidentally hurt feelings. The employees saw her desire for improvement as a "nothing is ever good enough" mentality, and she sensed the team was losing momentum.

After carefully analyzing her approach, Anna-Vija realized that growth and development had to become part of WHO they were as a company. It couldn't just be her pointing out areas that needed improvement; everyone had to be involved. Anna-Vija changed her language during team meetings and began asking questions rather than making statements. "What's not working here? What could work even better?" she would ask. She urged her team to evaluate everything regularly and to openly share their thoughts, suggestions, and ideas with her and each other. When Anna-Vija stepped back to let the rest of her team contribute as she encouraged discussion and solicited feedback, she created a space where teammates were comfortable to point out where improvements could be made. When the focus was about progression of the company and not employee shortcomings, everyone was less threatened by criticism. It wasn't long before Anna-Vija's team came up with the slogan, "Don't get offended; get better." It became their motto and an ongoing reminder that they had to push each other to constantly evolve if they wanted to achieve the lofty goals they set for the company.

When organizational charts fade away and employees see themselves as partners on a journey of learning, then altruistic transparency, coaching, and knowledge sharing happen organically from a place of genuine support and love. Skip Prichard, leadership author, refers to it as a performance-enhancing culture. As Anna-Vija discovered, when the intention is progress and development, then feedback becomes less intimidating and more inviting.

When you create an environment that prioritizes constant improvement, it engages your people, keeps them motivated, and pushes them to excel.

Unfortunately, the term "feedback" has become tainted in business. It is often misused to disguise criticism or express frustration, which sometimes triggers a "fight or flight" response from an unsuspecting employee. Numerous studies report a coaching approach is a more effective and positive way to present growth opportunities.[59] While many managers claim they are great at coaching their employees, the reality is they are falling short. Research suggests the reason so many managers fail at coaching is because they don't really understand what it is.[60] They believe coaching is telling someone what to do when actually it is about helping the coachee find the solution. Coaching involves listening and asking powerful questions to ignite deep reflection,[61] all while keeping the focus on the other person. If you are coaching someone, you are focused on *their growth*, not yours, and you are listening to *their voice*, not your own.

Having the best possible capital doesn't happen by accident. If you want to attract and keep quality employees, you really have to be a quality employer. It takes managers acting as coaches. It takes leaders consistently paying attention to their people. It takes necessary and sufficient resources. A manager can't be a great coach one day and a total jerk the next. A supervisor can't spend a significant amount of time with one employee and completely neglect another. You can't expect to have the most educated employees around with no budget for employee training and education. It's not easy. It's a never-ending work in progress that requires time and effort. If it were simple, more companies would be doing it.

If you want to excel as an organization, every employee needs to be incessant about upping their game. They can't just maintain or they won't keep up. Organizational L.O.V.E. has to be the constant, so continuous learning will spark engagement and fuel purpose within your people. If you want to make change, you can't get sucked into traps other companies fall into. You can't get complacent or take shortcuts. To develop a roster of the best possible people, make a conscious decision to avoid the most common pitfalls of management:

Make the Investment

As we've said throughout this book, your people require your ongoing time and attention. Period. You have to make spending time with them a priority. When your coworkers aren't pushing hard enough to achieve the goals they've set, be thoughtful and uplifting. Have the patience to coach them through obstacles and walk with them through failures. Stay outwardly focused on your people, be giving of yourself and your time, and share your knowledge regularly. This can be especially difficult when you are drowning in things to do but you have to remember, no matter how busy you are, your people need you! They crave your attention and need your guidance!

Let Feedback Be Fluid

Don't allow feedback to become the big scary monster that only comes out during annual reviews. We believe employees should always know where they stand because they are receiving regular feedback from supervisors. Younger generations desire and expect to hear ongoing assessments of their performance as they continuously evolve and progress. Weave both positive and constructive feedback into the daily conversation with your people. Keep growth and improvement at the crux of each interaction so you can change the attitude of your people from fearing feedback to being fueled by it.

You Don't Have to Be an A-Hole

If I'm being honest, I hate holding people accountable. I want to be the upbeat, encouraging manager who is cheering on my people, not busting them up when they miss a deadline or don't follow through on a project. But I learned something from Jackie: holding people accountable doesn't have to be a negative thing. At our clubs, every employee is required to wear a name tag as part of his or her uniform, and if you don't have your name tag on, Jackie will bust you. But instead of saying, "Where is your name tag!?" with a frustrated look and tone, she says, "Good morning, Nancy with no name tag. How are you today?" in the most genuine and cheerful voice with a big smile on her face. What is amazing is that Nancy knows that she needs to get her name tag on pronto, but it isn't the entire focus of the interaction.

Jackie rightly points out that holding people accountable doesn't mean you have to be an energy-sucking A-hole! Accountability is really about helping your people meet expectations and play their best game. So if you don't hold them accountable, they aren't reaching their potential. Be persistent and keep your people focused on what they need to do to achieve excellence. You can be kind and positive when you do it, but don't believe that you are doing anyone any favors when you avoid pointing out that Nancy isn't wearing her name tag.

This can be especially tricky when you have close relationships with your coworkers. Just because you feel like your coworkers are your friends doesn't mean you make excuses for them or pretend like you didn't notice that something was wrong. Give honest feedback, give tough love when it's warranted, and have difficult conversations. As we've gone to a higher percentage of remote working, companies might be finding that challenging. Still, it's important to constantly connect and be honest, even if it feels uncomfortable. Just like being a parent, sometimes you have to hold up the mirror to help someone see their true reality. Begin every conversation by saying that you have the other person's best interests in mind; then the focus becomes more on development and improvement and less about shortcomings or personal conflict. Be relentless about pushing everyone to be their very best.

Promote with Caution

When you have great people who are operating with excellence, it's easy to fall victim to the Peter Principle. This theory states employees will continue to rise in the organizational hierarchy through promotion until they reach a level of respective incompetence.[62] The problem is not necessarily that the wrong people are being promoted, but more likely that the people doing the promoting are doing it all wrong. Case in point: a recent study by CareerBuilder revealed that 58 percent of managers say they never received any kind of management training.[63]

I've inherited more Peters than I'd like to admit. I recall Katy, who was a fantastic server. All the members loved her, so when the dining room manager took another job, Katy was a shoe-in replacement to avoid wasting time and money recruiting and hiring a new manager. When I began working at the club and observed Katy's managing ability, I quickly discovered that the club had lost a great server and gained a poor manager. Katy hadn't been adequately trained and didn't know how to manage people other than through fear. She used the "you better listen to me or else" tactic, which created a toxic workplace. Instead of earning respect, she demanded it, which had the opposite desired result.

Promoting from within often fails, because promoting a person doesn't mean you *improve* the person! Believing Katy understood the new position's duties and responsibilities was an assumption that led to disaster. Katy needed to be *fully trained* for her new role, just like a new employee. The promoted employee needs just as much time, attention, and resources as a brand-new one. You have to take them back to Day One where the onboarding and training process begins. That is where so many managers get it wrong. Just because Katy knows where the bathroom is and knows how the company works does not mean she knows how to handle her new role.

Avoid the Peter Principle by identifying the real reason you are promoting an employee. If it's to save time or to keep that employee happier longer, you might want to rethink your decision. Consider starting small by adding "bite-sized" responsibilities to an employee you are thinking about promoting. See how he or she handles the additional responsibility and proceed from there. If you do promote the person, don't hang them out to dry! Walk with the promotee through the process, coaching and guiding along the way, and be diligent to give him or her all the knowledge, training, skill development, resources, and support necessary for success.

Investing in your people will become even more important as the competition for jobs continues to climb. Skills considered necessary for workers will also continue to evolve, dictated by advances in technology. The best way to sustain your company's future is to reduce turnover and retain your valuable employees! What's the best way to do that? Give them what they want: Coaching! Development! Growth opportunity! A lot of companies *talk* about providing advanced training and education and *say* that they prioritize employee growth, but few actually deliver to the degree that workers need and expect. Training and development is expensive, time consuming, and requires employees to be away from their normal daily tasks. It adds another complex layer to the operation, which is why companies that do it well are admired. According to *HR Magazine*, companies that invest at least $1,500 in training per employee can see an average of 24 percent more profit than companies that invest less.[64]

Marriott is recognized around the world for prioritizing employee development in all of its hotel properties, especially for managers. There is definitely a correlation between its extensive manager training and the fact that the average tenure of Marriott hotel general managers is twenty-five years![65] That is far above the industry norm. The company has been on *Fortune's* list of Best Companies to Work For every year since the list's inception, reaffirming the fact that employees desire to be invested in! Make upskilling, reskilling, and new-skilling common in your organization by always preparing workers for their next jobs. Teach your people the important hard and soft skills they need today and will need in the future. Prioritize and reinforce every employee's ability to keep learning![66]

THE PATH TO THRIVING

I think it's obvious by now that when your organization is thriving, your employees are happier! Engaged employees learn more, care more, work more, and perform better. As a result, customers are happier—and that is the ultimate goal! It's why we believe the old slogan is absolutely true:

Happy Employees = Happy Customers.

If you think employee happiness is a bunch of bologna—think again. Research indicates that happy employees deliver 31 percent higher productivity, demonstrate three times higher creativity on the job, and are ten times more engaged in their work! They also generate 37 percent greater sales figures and are three times more satisfied with their jobs.[67] Happy employees put their hearts into what they do. Remember, *value* begets *value*! Those who are Cared for with heart put their heart back into their job. In other words, those who are *invested in* by the company *invest themselves* in the company. This is when excellence comes to fruition.

Excellence is really about influence. When you meet an employee for the first time during an interview, you leave an impact as to how they will be treated, respected, and Cared for. When the employee arrives for the first day on the job, you shape their behavior going forward. This continues through every aspect of the five steps and comes full circle, because when you Care, it becomes tangible and you can see it and feel it so much so that the employees then influence others. They are positive change agents for each other, the customers, and the community. When employees achieve influence, they achieve excellence!

But the glory of Pure Human Connection doesn't stop with excellence; it's merely the launchpad to a thriving organization…

ONE VS. ONE

The Rolling Stones, one of the most famous rock bands in the world, was formed in the 1960s and has captivated fans with its music for over fifty years. With more than 250 million records sold, the Rolling Stones has been categorized as one of the 100 Greatest Artists of All Time. If you've ever seen them perform, it's obvious that each member of the band operates with pure excellence. The Stones practice endlessly and for at least two months before going on tour to make sure they are able to perform with almost telepathic communication. It is their ridiculously close connection that has kept this band together for so many years. Their unique personalities, talents, and strengths allow each band member to freely perform as a master rocking his instrumental craft, yet it is their tremendously close bond that transcends their musical creations to a level that electrifies audiences. This special connection is what makes it possible for guitarist Keith Richards to communicate the need to speed up the tempo of a song with just a single glance to rhythm guitarist Ronnie Wood. "The band performs as a seamless unit, each individual listening and responding to others in what Wood calls a conversation through music," wrote Khoi Tu, author of *Superteams: The Secrets of Stellar Performance from Seven Legendary Teams.* Offstage, each band member plays a very specific role for the team: Richards is their spiritual leader, Woods is the mediator, Charlie Watts is the band's backbone, and Mick Jagger acts as a sort of chief executive.[68] The Rolling Stones' ability to operate with excellence both on and off stage, combined with their intense cohesion, is what creates the magnetic force and transforms the band into a Superteam, according to Tu.

The Rolling Stones didn't become a legendary rock band just by being excellent musicians. They became renowned worldwide by having the right people in the right places at the right times doing the right things. It is their unique chemistry that has sustained the band's success for more than fifty years!

A common phrase in the sports world is "team chemistry," and it has become a popular term noted in performance analytics across many industries. Team chemistry is the secret sauce; it's the unique bond that unifies a team. Phil Jackson, the former Chicago Bulls coach, said he was always looking for "what creates the bonds" between players to give them the competitive advantage. Jackson strongly believes that "it's the alchemy that can turn teammates into champions," reported the *Harvard Business Review*.[69]

When individuals work together with a shared sense of purpose, a feeling of camaraderie, and a deep investment in each other's success, team members feel more secure, more confident, and more devoted. Happiness, influence, and team chemistry are all results that come from the five steps of Pure Human Connection. These might seem like fluff in the business world because they are intangible and sometimes hard to define, but we believe they are very necessary components to thriving. The Rolling Stones have been thriving for more than five decades! It's why we say that when every player is operating with individual excellence, the team can ascend to higher levels, because they are so deeply connected that they truly operate as *ONE*. A company begins to thrive when the whole becomes greater than the sum of its parts.

BETTER TOGETHER

Have you ever watched a US Navy SEAL team breach a target? It's like a perfectly choreographed dance that is quite impressive. When they enter a room, the first guy in covers 45 degrees, the second covers the next 45 degrees, and so on until 360 degrees are covered in 45-degree chunks by each member of the team, which moves as one fluid unit. "There's no way, no matter how good I am, that I can cover 360 degrees alone. But when we do it as a team, each person takes 45 degrees and we can conquer anything," said Curt Cronin, a former SEAL. "We can walk into a new environment, in the worst of conditions, against an enemy in their home environment and we can win."

Navy SEALs know that their chance of survival is significantly greater when the group functions as a team. It is not individuals being great at what they do next to others being great at what they do, it's the *team* covering ground and encountering obstacles while operating at a very high level bonded together. That is thriving! There are no holes. Where one team member falls short, another is there to fill in the gaps. It's on target. It's efficient. It's intense communication. When an organization is thriving, it can overcome even the gravest of challenges.

The most horrible thing any of my teams and I ever had to endure was when a mother was killed at our club's swimming pool. It was a gray and rainy summer Sunday. A synchronized swim meet was scheduled for late morning that typically drew a crowd of fifty people or so. It was a fairly quiet day at the club, so I went to visit some friends an hour away. It was early afternoon when I got the call. Matt, our pool snack bar manager, a recent high school graduate, was frantic on the other end of the phone. I thought he was playing a prank on me when he told me that a giant tree limb had fallen and landed on a mom and her nine-year-old daughter, just missing several other bystanders. Matt, noticeably shaken and with tears in his voice, told me it was no joke. The family was enjoying the swim meet alongside the pool when there was a sudden loud crack, followed by a crash. A nearly two-foot-in-circumference tree branch had snapped and fallen from one of the recently inspected hundred-year-old oak trees that outlined the pool area. The daughter was able to climb free of the limb with just a few scratches, but her mother was crushed underneath. She was killed instantly. My mind raced as he asked me what he should do because all the snack bar and lifeguard staff, mostly high school kids, were crying or in shock.

As I walked through the pool area an hour later, I didn't know how we would ever be the cheery, upbeat club where families came to have fun again. The next day, I picked up the phone with shaking hands. I was dreading calling the husband with every fiber of my being. I was terrified he would confirm what I already knew: his wife's death was my fault. It happened at my club; I was responsible. What I didn't expect was my apology and condolences to be interrupted with his gratitude, "Three, thank you so much for everything you are doing. I hope you know this was a freak accident and in no way should you blame yourself for what happened." Tears poured down my face as a weight was lifted off my chest.

The next day, I gathered the management team to tell them about my phone call and fought back tears as I encouraged each teammate to let go of the guilt we were carrying. We all felt responsible and yet helpless for what our member family was enduring. The days that followed produced some of the most incredible moments of healing I've ever experienced. Everyone at our club was dealing with the tragedy in different ways and at different paces. At times, we saw one another break down, choke up, or quickly walk away. Employees comforted one another and lifted each other up. Every one of us was hurting, and we felt better by helping each other feel better. We were understanding, patient, and encouraging at a whole new level. Through therapy sessions, counseling, team meetings, hugs, and a lot of love and support, our team rose from the depths of despair stronger than ever. In honor of the life we lost, we became closer, more deeply connected, and better for what we had gone through together.

After experiencing a death at our club, our whole team had a different perspective. When we encountered a problem, we simply worked through it. Our team had discovered that it didn't matter what we faced—we knew we had each other's backs and that we could persevere as long as we did it together. It might not be as extreme as the Navy SEALs nodding to one another to say "my life in yours and yours in mine" before they jump out of a helicopter, but when employees are emotionally connected to one another, they feel a stronger sense of purpose and responsibility to do more for their teammates, with their teammates…and that's when thriving takes hold.

TRANSITIONING FROM A TEAM TO A TRIBE

When teammates are deeply bonded and the five steps of connection are in place, something meaningful and almost magical takes place. Authenticity, realness, vulnerability, and empathy are foundational pillars of any team; it is refreshing, exciting, and fulfilling to all those who are part of it. But in order to reach the state of thriving in your organization, you must have Pure Human Connection, which establishes deeper bonds, almost like a tribe.

Rich Handler, the CEO of a financial group called Jefferies, wrote a letter to his teammates each month to encourage and inspire them. One particular letter shared a message from Clint Bruce, a retired Navy SEAL officer and former NFL player, during a leadership program. Bruce emphasized the importance of thinking like a tribe as opposed to a team, and he detailed the significant difference in the two mindsets:

"A team is a collection of people all working for a common goal. A tribe is a collection of people who know why they are together, are passionate about each other, bleed for a unified common cause and trust each other implicitly. Tribes are fearless, selfless, fully committed and tireless in pursuing their unified goals. Tribes are lean, efficient, move quickly and quietly, and get the job done. Tribes Care about each other's well-being and collective success. Tribes pick each other up every time. Tribes are always honest with each other and can always give and take constructive criticism. Tribes never have false agendas and speak plainly, openly and with integrity in purpose."[70]

Everything we've covered in this book has been building to this definition of a tribe. Tribes think, behave, and feel differently than teams, and their work yields different results. Tribes thrive! The hearts of tribe members are imprinted by the connections and experiences gained from the tribe. Their lives are enriched!

Would you quit a job where you genuinely loved the people you worked with? Would you phone it in for a boss who constantly made an investment in your skills, knowledge, and well-being? Would you work tirelessly for a job that truly enhances your life? Ask yourself, are you ready to take the final step and become a tribe? Then throw out the old-school hierarchical organizational charts. If you want to thrive, establish a nucleus and protect it with everything you've got!

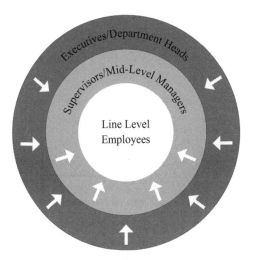

Tribes embrace the L.O.V.E. model where every level of the organization is supporting the next "layer" inward. In a traditional organizational chart, everything is either moving up or down. In this model, executives and department heads work to support the supervisors and mid-level managers, who work to support the line-level employees. The inner-most circle is the most coveted and nurtured layer of the organization. We call it "the Nucleus."

A Nucleus is defined as "the center and most important part of an object or group forming the basis for its activity and growth." It's also known as the hub, heart, core, crux, or focal point. The Nucleus is the core of the organization because the line-level employees are the ones who are leaving lasting impressions on customers. Rather than look at these employees as merely the underlings for those higher up in the company, we see them as crucial people that make or break the company! At the line level, every decision and action is multiplied. When each layer of the company makes taking Care of the next tier their utmost priority, it sets the organization in motion. Unlike the old org charts, in this model there is no beginning, no end, no top or bottom.

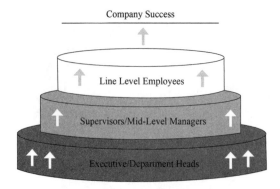

The L.O.V.E. model results in a thriving tribe because each layer is lifting up the next level, pushing the whole organization to new heights. It represents all of the five steps, in different stages and at different paces, yet all moving and working together. Yes, there's still a hierarchy, but we are obsessed with this depiction because it isn't about stepping on others to lift yourself higher as you climb up the ranks. Instead, the L.O.V.E. model is encompassing, inclusive, compassionate, and never ending. It represents the notion that when every person is focused on helping those around them win, everyone wins!

The cycle of connection cannot be broken, but it does require consistency to be effective. In our research, we've found many CEOs quickly get on board with our process, but it's the level of management below them that often struggles to give up power or doesn't fully understand the goal, and consequently the entire entity suffers. When each layer of the organization operates wholeheartedly by always focusing on the next layer in, the encircling effect is all about encouragement, inclusion, knowledge sharing, and support. It creates a cohesive group, a unified purpose, and a powerful connectivity. It becomes about lifting each other up with love!

This is why thriving companies are crushing the competition. It's why thriving organizations are being flooded with résumés and bombarded by people who want to work there. When your company is being fueled by love, there is nothing in the world like it! There is no other force on this planet stronger than a connected group of people who have a vision to see the goal, who know where they are going, and who are totally Committed to achieving the result together. We have had the great fortune to be part of these extremely connected workforces, and they have been some of the most extraordinary experiences of our lives! The bonds that we formed have lasted to this day, even though we haven't seen or spoken to some of our former colleagues for some time. One of the most sacred and rewarding gifts you can give is the rare gift of deep connection, unity, and love. And when you create it, you present the ultimate win-win situation, because together, you can accomplish anything.

The Fourth of July was our largest event of the year. We were expecting nearly two thousand people for an evening of festivities, music, food, and fireworks. Our transition at the club in Dallas was almost complete, as we were finally operating at a high level and working as a unified team. By lunchtime, we were so far ahead of our event setup schedule that a group of us managers sat down to lunch with our interns. The conversation was lighthearted and we all felt really good about how smoothly everything was going. At 3:00, the other sixty employees checked in, were assigned their tasks, and went to work putting the final touches on the setup for what we were sure would be the easiest event we'd ever executed. We were ready. Or so we thought.

At 3:45, one little dark cloud, not even enough to put a blip on the radar, found its way over the club and unleashed a torrential downpour that lasted more than thirty minutes. We stood, frozen in horror, as the hundreds of perfectly set and patriotically decorated tables covering the patio, lawn, and golf course were destroyed by the buckets of rain that fell from the sky—a sky that just moments before was clear and perfectly sunny. The games, inflatables, balloons, and festive décor were pelted with driving rain as the DJ frantically raced to cover his equipment and escape the cascades of water.

Jackie grabbed the other managers and came running to find me to determine what we were going to do. "Three, what's the plan?" she asked. I said what I was truly thinking: "It's over. We're dead. This is a catastrophe." I stood watching the rain hammer our flawlessly decorated lawn covered in red, white, and blue tables. Centerpieces, table numbers, salt and pepper shakers, rolled silverware, and hundreds of chairs were soaked. All I could do was stare out the window and try to calm my overwhelming sense of nausea. Jackie stared at me, waiting for my energetic, confident self to return with a brilliant plan, but it didn't happen. I was crushed, and I literally did not know what to do.

After a few minutes, Jackie nearly pushed me into my office, where she stood fuming mad. "Three, get it together! We can't just give up, we can do this!" My bleak face proved she wasn't getting through to me. "Three, they need you. We need you to be our leader, our inspiration, and our cheerleader that we can accomplish anything. We can fix this!" she yelled. I sat in my office quietly as she stormed out.

Refusing to give up, Jackie quickly rallied the managers and told them to gather every employee on the property for a meeting ASAP. Lifeguards, cooks, housekeepers, waitstaff, security guards, and bartenders all stood there in disbelief. I stepped in front of the group and found myself saying, "I don't know how this could happen. There was no rain in the forecast. There was nothing on the radar. Two thousand people will arrive in less than two hours and..." My voice trailed off as I made eye contact with Jackie. I remembered her words and said, "Guys, this was not part of the plan, but it happened. It's up to us to turn things around. The people in this room last year at this time couldn't have pulled this off, but you guys, you are why I know we can do this!"

It was then that Jackie jumped up on a chair so that everyone could see her and she began rattling off instructions and assigning groups tasks. "Here's what we're going to do. Lifeguards, grab the laundry cart. You guys can go out right now in your swimsuits and start pulling the wet tablecloths off in the rain. Housekeepers, start getting new linens ready and collect as many towels as you can find. As soon as it stops raining, head out and start wiping tables and chairs!" After everyone had been assigned a job, they jumped up and sprang into action. I watched what looked like dozens of mice scurrying in different directions. Within twenty minutes, the rain stopped and a mass of employees wearing every kind of uniform possible descended on the lawn. Jackie was the orchestrator, directing employees and hollering "Way to go! Keep it up!" and "We only have forty more minutes!" Jenny and Hannah, drenched from carrying wet piles of silverware, quickly established an assembly line where two thousand rolls of silverware could be unrolled, washed, dried, and rerolled in minutes. It had taken dozens of employees days to make them in the first place. Throughout the chaos, I heard all different voices shouting "Great job guys!" "We can do it!" and "Teamwork wins!" Housekeepers were working beside lifeguards and security guards were working with chefs. At one point, my mouth dropped when I saw the DJ, not an employee but a vendor we had hired for the day, amid the group of employees frantically helping to roll silverware! When I told him he didn't have to help, he answered, "Are you kidding? I want to help! I just want to be part of this!"

As the clock ticked to 5:48, the last of the chairs were being wiped down and the final pieces of silverware were being reset. Our first members arrived just moments later and asked if we'd had rain. They lived two blocks away and hadn't seen a drop! Our bad luck!

But somehow, we turned our misfortune into the most amazing experience. Yes, it was stressful, intense, and organized chaos, but we did it. Together. Coworkers were hugging and slapping high fives. We were exhausted, soaked, and yet somehow reenergized for what we had just accomplished. Every person had a role, but when a crisis hit, titles, departments, and uniforms didn't matter. Each employee knew our goal. The tasks themselves were irrelevant; people saw what needed to be done and they did it. We weren't departments working next to other departments, we were operating as ONE. When one employee needed help, another jumped in to assist. When one employee had a question, another was eager to answer it. We were thriving!

Thriving is when everyone steps up…when every person knows what needs to be done and finds a way to make it happen. Thriving is when you accomplish things you thought you'd never be able to do. It's when you are *loyal* to the people around you, embracing *ownership*, producing *value*, and operating with *excellence*. It's when the bonds between each other are so powerful that they produce a renewed sense of strength. Thriving is when you lift each other up, carry each other across the finish line, and believe in someone else until they can believe in themselves.

You see, when you create this kind of tribe in your organization, you will discover that it's not only about hiring talented people or just being great at recognizing achievements. It's about loving, respecting, and trusting your people enough to take your organization to the best possible place and then rewarding them for it. When you do, your people will see that it's not about flipping hamburgers, washing cars, cutting grass, or mopping floors. They will see that it's not about WHAT they are doing, it's about HOW they are doing it and WHO they are doing it with. It's about serving each other and working together to accomplish something bigger than themselves. Purpose is what brings people together, and when you bring purpose into an environment where people are Cared for, trusted, respected, supported, and loved, it's not about the service you are providing or the product you are building. It's about loving what you do, the people you do it with, and the organization for whom you work. We've all probably worked at neat places, had impressive job titles, and created notable results, yet the thing that remains long after we've left are the relationships and the connections we've made with people over the years. That is where the LOVE lives on, forever enriching our lives.

***

Now that you've read this book…what are you going to do about it?

How will you spark change in your organization? Do you have the courage to look deep in the mirror and ask yourself, "Am I the leader I want to be? Am I proud of who I am?" The answers…and the path ahead…are in your hands. You have the power to embrace the People First mindset to build relationships and create opportunities for Pure Human Connection within your company. Be the leader who inspires, who lifts others up and brings L.O.V.E. into your business. It is time to reinvent what success looks like. Are you ready to lead your team to unexplored heights while building a legacy that is sure to last? Begin the exciting, enriching journey to create a life-changing People First environment by genuinely caring for, supporting, and loving your fellow workers. Then watch your organization and all of its people THRIVE!

It begins with YOU!

ENDNOTES

1   Rick Kiley, "Gallup Report: Time to Reinvent Employee Recognition," GThankYou! Certificates of Gratitude, February 20, 2017, https://www.gthankyou.com/blog/gallup-claims-time-to-reinvent-employee-recognition. Accessed October 15, 2019.

2   Jena McGregor, "Group of Top CEOs says maximizing shareholder profits no longer can be the primary goal of corporations," The Washington Post, August 19, 2019, https://www.washingtonpost.com/business/2019/08/19/lobbying-group-powerful-ceos-is-rethinking-how-it-defines-corporations-purpose. Accessed October 15, 2019.

3   Lori Goler, Janelle Gale, Brynn Harrington, and Adam Grant, "Why People Really Quit Their Jobs," Harvard Business Review, January 11, 2018, https://hbr.org/2018/01/why-people-really-quit-their-jobs. Accessed February 21, 2020.

4   John Kotter, "Does corporate culture drive financial performance?" Forbes, February 10, 2011, https://www.forbes.com/sites/johnkotter/2011/02/10/does-corporate-culture-drive-financial-performance/?sh=39cb6e177e9e. Accessed April 29, 2021.

5   "The John Deere Journal," John Deere, https://johndeerejournal.com. Accessed April 29, 2021.

6   Russell Pearlman, Karen Kane, and Hazel Euan-Smith, "CEOs Are Betting Technology Will Rule, But Are They Ignoring Their Most Important Asset?" Briefings Magazine, Issue 30: The Future of Work, https://www.kornferry.com/content/dam/kornferry/docs/article-migration/Briefings30_Feature_Future_28-37.pdf. Accessed April 29, 2021.

7   Joanne Koo, "The Future of Work is Human," Joanne Koo's Blog, August 29, 2017, https://joannekoosg.com/2017/08/29/the-future-of-work-is-human. Accessed October 17, 2019.

8   Russell Pearlman, Karen Kane, and Hazel Euan-Smith, "CEOs Are Betting Technology Will Rule, But Are They Ignoring Their Most Important Asset?" Briefings Magazine, Issue 30: The Future of Work, https://www.kornferry.com/content/dam/kornferry/docs/article-migration/Briefings30_Feature_Future_28-37.pdf. Accessed April 29, 2021.

9   Russell Pearlman, Karen Kane, and Hazel Euan-Smith, "CEOs Are Betting Technology Will Rule, But Are They Ignoring Their Most Important Asset?" Briefings Magazine, Issue 30: The Future of Work, https://www.kornferry.com/content/dam/kornferry/docs/article-migration/Briefings30_Feature_Future_28-37.pdf. Accessed April 29, 2021.

10   Amy Adkins, "Millennials: The Job-Hopping Generation," Gallup, May 12, 2016, https://www.gallup.com/workplace/231587/millennials-job-hopping-generation.aspx. Accessed April 29, 2021.

11   G. I. Sanders, "Employee Productivity Statistics: Everything You Need to Know in 2020," Dynamic Signal, March 6, 2020, https://dynamicsignal.com/2020/03/06/employee-productivity-statistics-2020/. Accessed April 29, 2021.

12   Cigna Newsroom, "Cigna Takes Action To Combat The Rise Of Loneliness And Improve Mental Wellness In America," Cigna.com, January 23, 2020, https://www.cigna.com/about-us/newsroom/news-and-views/press-releases/2020/cigna-takes-action-to-combat-the-rise-of-loneliness-and-improve-mental-wellness-in-america. Accessed April 29, 2021.

13   Dale Buss, "CEO Chapman Spreads Gospel of 'Truly Human Leadership' Beyond Manufacturing," Chief Executive, April 15, 2019, https://chiefexecutive.net/ceo-chapman-human-leadership-manufacturing. Accessed April 29, 2021.

14   Patrick W. Watson, "Why Businesses Must Double Down On Humans Instead Of Technology," Forbes, April 25, 2018, https://www.forbes.com/sites/patrickwwatson/2018/04/25/why-businesses-must-double-down-on-humans-instead-of-technology/?sh=24ccaa165814. Accessed April 29, 2021.

15   Eric Ransdell, "The Nike Story? Just Tell It!" Fast Company, December 31, 1999, https://www.fastcompany.com/38979/nike-story-just-tell-it. Accessed April 29, 2021.

16   Knowledge@Wharton, "Wisdom at Work: Why the Modern Elder Is Relevant," Wharton University of Pennsylvania, January 24, 2019, https://knowledge.wharton.upenn.edu/article/wisdom-workplace-modern-elder-relevant. Accessed April 29, 2021.

17   Dana Manciagli, "How your company can survive the baby boomer brain drain," bizwomen, January 31, 2017, https://www.bizjournals.com/pacific/bizwomen/news/profiles-strategies/2017/01/how-your-company-can-survive-the-baby-boomer-brain.html?page=all. Accessed April 29, 2021.

18   Brene Brown, "Brene Brown Definitions," BreneBrown.Com, last modified 2021, https://brenebrown.com/definitions/#close-popup. Accessed June 4, 2019.

19   "Red Venture Reviews," Glassdoor.com, last modified April 28, 2021, https://www.glassdoor.com/Reviews/Red-Ventures-Reviews-E142090_P4.htm. Accessed June 2020.

20   Glassdoor Team, "50 HR & Recruiting Stats that Make You Think," Glassdoor for Employers, January 20, 2015, https://www.glassdoor.com/employers/blog/50-hr-recruiting-stats-make-think. Accessed March 12, 2016.

21   Glassdoor Team, "Building an Employer Brand from Scratch," Glassdoor for Employers, June 1, 2018, https://www.glassdoor.com/employers/blog/how-to-create-an-employer-brand-from-scratch. Accessed December 2, 2018.

22 "About," Kickstarter, https://www.kickstarter.com/about. Accessed May 12, 2020.

23 Erika Fry, "Can Levi's Make Life Better for Garment Workers?" Fortune.com, September 8, 2017, http://fortune.com/2017/09/08/levis-change-the-world, Accessed 2017.

24 Erika Fry, "Can Levi's Make Life Better for Garment Workers?" Fortune.com, September 8, 2017, http://fortune.com/2017/09/08/levis-change-the-world. Accessed 2017.

25 Chris Arnold, "Fired Wells Fargo Employees Allege Attempts To Blow The Whistle," NPR, October 14, 2016, https://www.npr.org/2016/10/14/497991242/fired-wells-fargo-employees-allege-attempts-to-blow-the-whistle. Accessed February 4, 2018.

26 SAS, "Our Values," SAS.com, April 4, 2017, https://www.sas.com/en_us/company-information/values.html. Accessed May 23, 2017.

27 Laszlo Bock, "Here's Google's Secret to Hiring the Best People," Wired, April 7, 2015, https://www.wired.com/2015/04/hire-like-google. Accessed March 17, 2016.

28 "Calculating The Cost Of Employee Turnover," G&A Partners, June 3, 2016, https://www.gnapartners.com/resources/articles/how-much-does-employee-turnover-really-cost-your-business. Accessed April 29, 2021.

29 Moritz Plassnig, "5 Reasons Why Hiring is the Single Most Important Skill for Founders," Entrepreneur, February 5, 2016, https://www.entrepreneur.com/article/254430. Accessed March 28, 2016.

30 Tim Yocum, "How We Stopped Reviewing Resumes and Started Making Better Hires," Fast Company, September 21, 2015, https://www.fastcompany.com/3051257/how-we-stopped-reviewing-resumes-started-ed-making-better-hires. Accessed February 25, 2016.

31 Cassidy Leventhal, "Resumes Are a Terrible Way to Hire People," yahoo!finance, February 22, 2020, https://finance.yahoo.com/news/resumes-terrible-way-hire-people-130022433.html. Accessed April 29, 2021.

32 Sarah Young, "Gut Feelings Really Do Stop You From Making Mistakes, Study Finds," Independent, March 23, 2018, https://www.independent.co.uk/life-style/gut-feelings-instinct-stop-mistakes-brain-signal-influence-emotions-study-findings-a8270611.html. Accessed June 30, 2020.

33 Sue Shellenbarger, "Job-Interview Etiquette Isn't Just for the Applicants," The Wall Street Journal, July 8, 2019, https://www.wsj.com/articles/job-interview-etiquette-isnt-just-for-the-applicants-11562578204?mod=searchresults&page=1&pos=1. Accessed July 14, 2019.

34 Shelley MacDougall and Kevin MacDonald, "The Extraordinary Leader Master Call - Extraordinary Service," October 19, 2017.

35 "Nearly Three in Four Employers Affected by a Bad Hire, According to a Recent CareerBuilder Survey," CareerBuilder, December 7, 2017, http://press.careerbuilder.com/2017-12-07-Nearly-Three-in-Four-Employers-Affected-by-a-Bad-Hire-According-to-a-Recent-CareerBuilder-Survey. Accessed April 29, 2021.

36 "Glassdoor Resource Library for Hiring and Recruiting," Glassdoor for Employers, last modified April 2021, https://www.glassdoor.com/employers/topics/hiring-recruiting. Accessed December 14, 2018.

37 Kate Davidson, "Employers Find 'Soft Skills' Like Critical Thinking in Short Supply," The Wall Street Journal, August 30, 2016, https://www.wsj.com/articles/employers-find-soft-skills-like-critical-thinking-in-short-supply-1472549400. Accessed April 29, 2021.

38 Adam Grant, "Unless You're Oprah, 'Be Yourself' Is Terrible Advice," The New York Times, June 4, 2016, https://www.nytimes.

com/2016/06/05/opinion/sunday/unless-youre-oprah-be-yourself-is-terrible-advice.html. Accessed April 29, 2021.

39 Tess Taylor, "Why do 28% of employees quit in their first 90 days? Poor onboarding practices," HRDrive, April 25, 2017, https://www.hrdive.com/news/why-do-28-of-employees-quit-in-their-first-90-days-poor-onboarding-practi/441139. Accessed June 5, 2017.

40 Ashley Autry, "2019 Employee Engagement & Loyalty Statistics," Access Perks, January 31, 2019, https://blog.accessperks.com/2019-employee-engagement-loyalty-statistics. Accessed May 5, 2020.

41 "Employee Training is Worth the Investment," go2HR, 2019, https://www.go2hr.ca/training-development/roi-of-training/employee-training-is-worth-the-investment. Accessed January 6, 2019.

42 Marianna Pogosyan, "In Helping Others, You Help Yourself," Psychology Today, May 30, 2018, https://www.psychologytoday.com/us/blog/between-cultures/201805/in-helping-others-you-help-yourself. Accessed October 20, 2020.

43 "Thrive Global," Thrive Global, https://thriveglobal.com. Accessed May 29, 2020.

44 "We're Retiring the 'Buffer Bootcamp' Period for New Teammates—Here's Why," Buffer, September 28, 2017, https://buffer.com/resources/45-day-period. Accessed November 18, 2018.

45 Ashley Autry, "2019 Employee Engagement & Loyalty Statistics," Access Perks, January 31, 2019, https://blog.accessperks.com/2019-employee-engagement-loyalty-statistics. Accessed May 5, 2020.

46 Chris Morris, "61 Million Gen Zers are about to enter the US workforce and radically change it forever," CNBC, May 2, 2018, https://www.cnbc.com/2018/05/01/61-million-gen-zers-about-to-enter-us-workforce-and-change-it.html. Accessed May 28, 2019.

47 "A conversation with Bill Walshe, CEO of Viceroy Hotels," Eloquence Magazine, Fall 2018.

48 "Jeff Weiner: Leading with Compassion," Super Soul–OWN Network, 2018.

49 Jacquelyn Smith, "17 Ways To Be Indispensable At Work," Forbes, September 5, 2013, https://www.forbes.com/sites/jacquelynsmith/2013/09/05/17-ways-to-be-indispensable-at-work/?sh=750c9710274d. Accessed April 29, 2021.

50 Kim Scott, "Micromanager, Absentee Manager or Thought Partner — Which One Are You?" Radical Candor, February 18, 2021, https://www.radicalcandor.com/micromanager. Accessed April 29, 2021.

51 David Rock, Jay Dixit & Barbara Steel, "How to Have Conversations that Make Employees Stay." April 1, 2019, https://qz.com/work/1583761/good-management-how-to-have-feedback-conversations-that-increase-employee-engagement/. Accessed May 20, 2021.

52 Marcel Schwantes, "Why Are Your Employees Quitting? A Study Says It Comes Down to Any of These 6 Reasons," Inc.com, October 23, 2017, https://www.inc.com/marcel-schwantes/why-are-your-employees-quitting-a-study-says-it-comes-down-to-any-of-these-6-reasons.html. Accessed April 29, 2021.

53 Julie Winkle Giulioni, "4 practices to foster psychological safety," SmartBrief, March 8, 2018, https://www.smartbrief.com/original/2018/03/4-practices-foster-psychological-safety. Accessed September 17, 2018.

54 Julie Winkle Giulioni, "4 practices to foster psychological safety," SmartBrief, March 8, 2018, https://www.smartbrief.com/original/2018/03/4-practices-foster-psychological-safety. Accessed September 17, 2018.

55 David Novak, "Recognizing Employees Is the Simplest Way to Improve Morale," Harvard Business Review, May 9, 2016, https://

hbr.org/2016/05/recognizing-employees-is-the-simplest-way-to-im-prove-morale. Accessed April 29, 2021.

56 Amy Morin, "How An Authentic 'Thank You' Can Change Your Workplace Culture," Forbes, November 20, 2016, https://www.forbes.com/sites/amymorin/2016/11/20/how-an-authentic-thank-you-can-change-your-workplace-culture/?sh=13ec1f827990. Accessed April 12, 2019.

57 Annamarie Mann and Nate Dvorak, "Employee Recognition: Low Cost, High Impact," Gallup, June 28, 2016, https://www.gallup.com/workplace/236441/employee-recognition-low-cost-high-impact.aspx. Accessed May 20, 2021.

58 Amy Adkins and Brandon Rigoni, "Millennials Want Jobs to Be Development Opportunities," Gallup, June 30, 2016, https://www.gallup.com/workplace/236438/millennials-jobs-development-opportunities.aspx. Accessed April 29, 2021.

59 Lori Goler, Janelle Gale, Brynn Harrington, and Adam Grant, "Why People Really Quit Their Jobs," Harvard Business Review, January 11, 2018, https://hbr.org/2018/01/why-people-really-quit-their-jobs. Accessed February 21, 2020.

60 Julia Milner and Trenton Milner, "Most Managers Don't Know How to Coach People. But They Can Learn," Harvard Business Review, last modified August 16, 2018, https://hbr.org/2018/08/most-managers-dont-know-how-to-coach-people-but-they-can-learn. Accessed November 9, 2018.

61 Julia Milner and Trenton Milner, "Most Managers Don't Know How to Coach People. But They Can Learn," Harvard Business Review, last modified August 16, 2018, https://hbr.org/2018/08/most-managers-dont-know-how-to-coach-people-but-they-can-learn. Accessed November 9, 2018.

62 Adam Hayes, "Peter Principle," Investopedia, last modified March 20, 2021, https://www.investopedia.com/terms/p/peter-principle.asp. Accessed April 29, 2021.

63 "More Than One-Quarter of Managers Said They Weren't Ready to Lead When They Began Managing Others, Finds New CareerBuilder Survey," CareerBuilder, March 28, 2011, http://press.careerbuilder.com/2011-03-28-More-Than-One-Quarter-of-Managers-Said-They-Werent-Ready-to-Lead-When-They-Began-Managing-Others-Finds-New-CareerBuilder-Survey. Accessed April 28, 2021

64 Jenna Conroy, "What is the cost of not training an employee?" Exude.com, June 20, 2018, https://www.exudeinc.com/blog/what-is-the-cost-to-not-training-an-employee. Accessed April 29, 2021.

65 "Marriott International Wins 2018 North American Candidate Experience Award by The Talent Board," Marriott International, December 17, 2018, https://news.marriott.com/news/2018/12/17/marriott-international-wins-2018-north-american-candidate-experience-award-by-the-talent-board. Accessed April 29, 2021.

66 Lauren Weber, "Why Companies Are Failing at Reskilling," Wall Street Journal, April 19, 2019, https://www.wsj.com/articles/the-answer-to-your-companys-hiring-problem-might-be-right-under-your-nose-11555689542. Accessed May 20, 2021.

67 Steve Nguyen, "A Positive Mindset and Happy Attitude Help You Succeed at Work," Workplace Psychology, March 8, 2012, https://workplacepsychology.net/2012/03/08/a-positive-mindset-and-happy-attitude-help-you-succeed-at-work. Accessed April 29, 2021.

68 Harvey Mackay, "The essentials of teamwork in the business world," StarTribune, September 20, 2020, https://www.startribune.com/the-essentials-of-teamwork-in-the-business-world/572457472. Accessed April 29, 2021.

69 Michael Schrage, "Team Chemistry Is the New Holy Grail of Performance Analytics," Harvard Business Review, March 5, 2014, https://

hbr.org/2014/03/team-chemistry-is-the-new-holy-grail-of-perfor-mance-analytics. Accessed April 29, 2021.

70 Julia La Roche, "JEFFERIES CEO: A former Navy SEAL made an incredible point to us about thinking like a 'tribe' instead of a 'team,'" Business Insider Australia, February 2, 2016, https://www.businessinsider.com.au/rich-handler-tribe-v-team-memo-to-jefferies-2016-2. Accessed April 29, 2021.

ACKNOWLEDGMENTS

First and foremost, Glory to God! He made this book possible and called us to put our ideas and philosophies in writing. His guidance is what got us through the tremendous process of writing this book! Looking back, God perfectly weaved people, places, and experiences into our lives and created every aspect of this book. It is His message, not ours, and we are so grateful for His work through us.

To our families...your love, support, and encouragement means the world to us. Thank you for believing in us and loving us every step of the way!

To our dear friend Tommy Spaulding, who encouraged us to write this book. We vividly remember the long walk in Florida where we shared our goals and dreams, and your immediate response helped make them a reality. Your support, assistance, and encouragement made it possible! Thank you for confidently believing there was a book "inside of us" and for helping us share our message. We are forever grateful to you!

To the magnificent Michael Palgon, our incredible agent...thank you for your saintlike patience! Poor Michael didn't know what he was getting into nearly five years ago when he agreed to work with us. We are certain this was one of the longest projects he has ever been a part of! Michael is a master of his craft, and we were so grateful to work with him. Michael, we are in awe of your amazing gift to "pull books out of people," and we feel so blessed that you shared your brilliance with us. Thank you (x100) for your time, effort, guidance, and friendship through this process.

To our friends, our current and former colleagues, and past interns... thank you for being our inspirations, our cheerleaders, and most importantly for enriching our lives with your presence. You have made our work light. You have been the reason we've been able to Do What We Do. You've fueled our passion, followed where we led, and loved us along the way. Thank you, thank you, thank you.

To Dorothy, our mother/mother-in-law, thank you for your editing expertise! We are lucky to have a brilliant editor in the family, and we are so appreciative of the endless hours you spent reviewing our work.

To our children…we wrote this with you in mind. It is our hope that your careers will be filled with caring bosses, supportive coworkers, and many people who put your success over their own. May you be loved for who you are both in and out of work.

To everyone who helped us in big and little ways to make this book possible…*thank you!* We know our lives have been blessed with THE BEST!

ABOUT THE AUTHORS

Three and Jackie Carpenter have spent their careers in the private club industry, where customer service must be at the highest level. With a track record for creating incredibly connected teams, upbeat work cultures, and thriving organizations, Three and Jackie develop and encourage employees to excel beyond their own expectations. The Carpenters have helped some of the most historic and respected country clubs become profitable, and have enriched the lives of hundreds of coworkers through the process. Coaching and cheering on students, interns, and young people early in their careers is their specialty.

Known for their enthusiasm and ability to connect people, Three and Jackie continue to work in the private club landscape. They speak and mentor others on the importance of People First in the business world. Both born and raised in Iowa, Three and Jackie are relatable, authentic, and passionate about helping others achieve their goals, enjoy their work, and lead fulfilled professional lives.

Website: www.ThreeandJackie.com
Facebook: ThreeAndJackie
Instagram: ThreeAndJackie
LinkedIn: Three-Jackie